THE GROCER'S
Granddaughter

THE GROCER'S Granddaughter

Ombersley Village During The 1940s

Rose Parish

LARGE PRINT

Oxford

942.47

First published in Great Britain 2007
by
Brewin Books Ltd.

Published in Large Print 2008 by ISIS Publishing Ltd.,
7 Centremead, Osney Mead, Oxford OX2 0ES
by arrangement with
Brewin Books Ltd.

British Library Cataloguing in Publication Data
Parish, Rose, 1937–
    The grocer's granddaughter. – Large print ed.
    (Isis reminiscence series)
    1. Parish, Rose, 1937– – Childhood and youth
    2. General stores – England – Ombersley – History
    – 20th century
    3. Country life – England – Ombersley – History
    – 20th century
    4. Large type books
    5. Ombersley (England) – Biography
    6. Ombersley (England) – Social life and customs –
    20th century
    I. Title
    942.4'40822'092

ISBN 978–0–7531–9482–9 (hb)
ISBN 978–0–7531–9483–6 (pb)

Printed and bound in Great Britain by
T. J. International Ltd., Padstow, Cornwall

For my granddaughter India Rose Parish.

Contents

PART TWO: VILLAGE PEOPLE

ACKNOWLEDGEMENTS

Thanks for your help in providing illustrations for this book . . . Arthur Turner and Ronald Shuard. Also to . . . John Silvester, for all his help, information and contributions, also for providing the Home Guard photograph and that of the old house at Turnmill and for his permission to use a copy of the painting of Turnmill as it was when the mill was working.

PREFACE

Ombersley is six miles north of Worcester, it is one of several settlements in the parish of the same name which now covers over 7,870 acres and is the third largest in Worcestershire, with a population of 2210 (2001 census). The parish, bounded by the rivers Severn and Salwarpe, and Hadley Brook, is one of the most fertile areas in the county.

In Roman times Ombersley was a forest clearing on a line of march north west from Worcester. There was a spring there providing a supply of fresh water and so it grew into an encampment. It was disafforested, as distinct from deforested, by Henry III in 1229. The name "Ombersley" is probably derived from Ambrosius, the name of a little known leader of the British resistance to Saxon invaders. It is mentioned in the Domesday Book records. There were two water mills, a couple of fishing weirs and several acres of meadow and arable land as well as two leagues of forest and a salt pan in Droitwich. The population was around 300 including 54 tenant farmers and two priests. In the 14th century Ombersley was granted the right to a weekly market and a four-day fair while the lease was owned by the Abbey of Evesham. This put it in line to develop into a town, but that has never happened.

The lease was taken over by the son of a former Bishop of Worcester, Sir Samuel Sandys who eventually bought the estate outright from James I for £2,000. At

Ombersley there remains archaeological evidence of Civil War fighting between Roundheads and Royalists along their trail to Worcester. The right to the church tithes was also acquired by the Sandys family when King Charles II sold it to them. They no longer collect the tithes, but the manor has remained the property of the Sandys family to the present time.

The Plague Stones, now placed near the island in the centre of the village by the Weighbridge building, used to be just outside the village on the Holt Fleet road. They are a reminder of the Black Death which swept the country in 1604. Food for travellers was left in them to prevent the travellers coming into contact with the villagers. There are other reminders of this medieval period in the growth of the village, including the 13th century remains of the original church, now the Sandys Mausoleum in St. Andrew's churchyard.

The 18th century agricultural revolution transformed farming methods; tools and equipment had been greatly improved, and enclosure of common land, crop rotation and selective breeding had been established. From 1870s, Ombersley became known as a market gardening and fruit growing area; this labour intensive form of agriculture was the main source of employment.

FOREWORD

This graphic picture of the Worcestershire village of Ombersley in the 1940s, seen through the eyes of childhood within a family running a busy village shop, makes fascinating reading. Set against the grim background of wartime and immediate post-war Britain with its ration books, restrictions and shortages of all kinds, this account of another world running in parallel with the sound of Flying Fortresses overhead and military convoys passing through Ombersley, paints a vivid scene of family life.

Especially resonant for those familiar with the period will be echoes of the part played by the BBC Home Service with its many very popular programme like ITMA.

Growing up with the presence of a grandmother near at hand adds another generation to the book, with her own fund of recollections and stories. As the threat of imminent invasion receded, D-Day passed, and a confident freedom grew and flourished, in the eventful world of village life.

This is a unique and closely observed record of Ombersley during a crucial decade. The author and all contributors to it deserve our warmest appreciation.

Lord Sandys

PART ONE:

VILLAGE LIFE

CHAPTER ONE

The Whys and Wherefores

I cannot claim to have begun life as a twinkle in anyone's eye. My story begins with the hasty marriage of my parents in 1936, my mother's age was 40 and my father was 45. There was a wintry chill in the air and no bells were rung. The marriage knot was swiftly and securely tied by a Registrar, no crowd of happy laughing guests were invited. Afterwards they went to a quiet elegant restaurant, champagne popped and quietly sparkled as they drank a toast, relaxed and ate a good meal listening to the pianist entertaining diners at a grand piano. A small "surprise" wedding cake topped with a spray of lily of the valley was presented to them when the coffee was served. After the wedding they set up home in a flat they had acquired in Rosemont Court, Rosemont Road, Acton, London W.1 opposite Rosemont Park.

My parents Florence B. Pester and Alfred L. Pryme, met in London in 1936. My mother was staying at a Ladies' Club in the Charing Cross area, where my father was Manager. My mother was treating herself to a short holiday before her next job. Until then she had worked first as a school-teacher, then as a private

3

governess for children of some very wealthy people and one (not so wealthy) Suffolk farmer. She enjoyed teaching, especially when she took residential posts as a governess; these provided very comfortable accommodation in lovely homes. She didn't have to concern herself with housework, cooking, laundry or household management, everything was provided.

My father, son of a Margate tailor, was trained in the hotel business before he joined the army in 1914 (aged 23) and served until the end of WWI as an officer's batman. He then returned to the hotel business Brighton and London and was fortunate to remain in full employment throughout the 1930s Depression. In later years he often spoke with nostalgia of those times. As a child, I used to love looking through his photograph albums with him; he always seemed to have pretty young ladies with him in and around his cars. He used to talk about taking his lady friends to plays and stage shows at various theatres in the West End and on outings to the seaside. I particularly remember him telling me of the times when he sat on the steps at the back of the club late at night, sharing cigarettes with a young actor named Laurence Olivier (1907-1989), who called himself "Larry". He met lots of interesting people and lived near to his family and friends.

My mother's pregnancy didn't cause any immediate problems, my father continued his job at the club, he kept his own bedroom there because he sometimes had to be on the premises overnight. Mother made friends with a widow named Mrs. Solomons and a single lady who she called Nancy, who worked for Methuen publishers in Essex Street; both these ladies had flats in Rosemont Court, and they enjoyed walking in the park together. My father had a car and when he was not working they visited his brothers and sister who lived in the London area. They were sometimes able to visit mother's parents in Ombersley to stay at the shop for a night or two.

My grandfather, John W. Pester and grandmother, Annie Pester had taken a lease on a village shop in Ombersley around 1928. Grandpa had sold his shop in West Bromwich to his brothers and his doctor suggested he should retire for the sake of his heart, so he found a less demanding business. They thought Ombersley was ideal, and changed the business to a general grocery store. Aunty Win, my mother's sister, came with them and helped in the shop.

Mother was *very* apprehensive about having a child at her age, so she came to stay at Ombersley for several weeks prior to my birth at a nursing home in Worcester on 10th July 1937. She returned to London after I arrived and they lived there happily until it became obvious that WWII was imminent.

WE MOVED TO OMBERSLEY

They considered it too dangerous to remain in London and arranged to move to Ombersley. My father applied for a job at 25 MU Hartlebury and was immediately accepted.

Mum and Daddy listened to BBC Home Service radio. The News at Nine o'clock was an important part of the day for them and most people at that time. They heard details of the Battle of Britain and Charles Gardner gave vivid accounts of the dogfights overhead. I can remember being told to "be quiet" when my parents were listening to Winston Churchill's stirring broadcasts. The Nazis used the British Fascist son of an Irish-born American, William Joyce, nicknamed "Lord Haw-Haw", to broadcast to Britain from Berlin. Hearing his somewhat sinister voice didn't help much at that time when people were anxious and worried about the invasion. The Ministry of Information were not very forthcoming, so some folk thought they would learn something from those broadcasts. They found No.1 Conygree Villas, at School Bank, Ombersley was available at an affordable rent, and moved in at the end of 1938.

Grandma and Grandpa were pleased to have us in the village. Mother started helping in the shop and I became the apple of my Grandpa's eye! Sadly he died when I was three years old, and Aunty Win married in the same year — 1940. I remember her pink wedding dress and the reception at The Crown & Sandys Hotel in the village.

It seemed that the war was going on all around our village, without ever encroaching into our midst. As far as I know air-raid shelters were not used in Ombersley. I do remember having to squeeze with my mother into the bottom of a big cupboard by the chimney-breast, when enemy aircraft were heard flying over. She said the chimney of a house usually remained even after bombing had destroyed the roof! My father didn't subscribe to that idea, and we didn't retreat to the cupboard many times. Only once did I sit with Grandma in the cellar at the shop when we heard sounds of aircraft at night.

The local ARP checked that every household had obeyed the blackout precautions in readiness for 1st September 1939 when it came into force. Thick curtains were hung up, people bought blackout paint, cardboard, brown paper and drawing pins — anything to blot out light in case it should help enemy bombers.

When bombs fell in places near to Ombersley the news spread very quickly. At the shop, customers kept my family up to date with the latest bombing events in Worcestershire. Many customers had family members or neighbours who were involved in transport and deliveries — the "grape vine" worked very well.

How were my parents going to cope with these huge changes in their lives?

CHAPTER
TWO

Ombersley Village

I unfold a picture of the village in the 1940s illustrating some of my formative years, the villagers and my family. The sun didn't shine all the time; people were not all good, kind or happy. Mine is a story of a village where the Victorian work ethic lived on, the lives of most villagers revolved around their work, and there was a collective will to keep going. For many that meant producing as much food as possible. Wages for manual workers were low, and all eligible men had been called up to fight the war. Working class people had to earn their livings, and had all been brought up to be thrifty and to live within their means. What they couldn't pay for they went without. At the family shop customers ran up very few outstanding debts, and people generally paid cash for their purchases and delivered orders. The main days for deliveries were Fridays and Saturdays. There were a few instances when orders were not paid for, sometimes because the man of the house hadn't brought his wages home. The goods were handed over in good faith, and the money was usually brought into the shop when they had it. Otherwise they would have been without their basic food rations for the weekend. There were rare instances when such a debt had to be written off, usually when the main wage earner succumbed to a long-term illness and the family could barely exist on the earnings of the wife with children.

Farm and estate workers who lived in tied cottages were in a slightly better position than those who had to pay rent to the Parish, or private landlords. In the years prior to 1945 there was no unemployment benefit, assistance for the disabled, child benefits, or state pensions. Everyone had to pay their own doctor's bills and medical expenses, which put a heavy load upon those with low incomes who had little or no savings. People were often too proud to ask for help, but the church did provide some assistance. The Beveridge Report of 1942 laid out the plan for *"Social Security from the cradle to the grave"*, and in 1945 at the end of WWII the Labour Government, under Clement Attlee, established this much needed system. It was however, 1948 before the National Health Service was implemented ensuring free medical, dental and health care for all.

Following the Church Act of 1814, Ombersley supported around a hundred people on continual benefit from parish rates money, and almost as many receiving intermittent relief. This was an ever increasing financial burden, therefore a workhouse[1] was built in the village and inmates arrived in 1827 — it was closed

---

[1] See more detailed information about the Workhouse in Ombersley at the end of Chapter 8.

in 1836. The aim had been to reduce the burden on local ratepayers, by housing around 24 inmates, mostly permanent residents. The workhouse in Hilltop Lane (formerly known as Hog Lane) stood empty for a time before being used as a private house, as it does today.

Ombersley joined the Droitwich Union when parish groups amalgamated to build large, bleak, austere workhouses for the poor and infirm. It is little wonder that there were always people who tramped the roads from one village to the next, and stayed, sometimes for long periods, in places where they could sleep in a barn or pigsty. I have heard many stories of such people, and others living in very inadequate conditions who were in fear and dread of having to go into a workhouse. They preferred to live that way, scrounging what food they could and earning small amounts from anyone who would give them work, rather than go into one of the workhouses.

After the fine, bright days of spring, the warmth of summer and autumn, open-air work and pleasures, the winter season began. Some folk welcomed the short days and dark nights. For them winter offered a comforting solidity, an opportunity for renewal and quiet restful activities. Grandma cooked warming stews with dumplings, made wholesome soup and used the heat from the *Triplex* oven to do plenty of baking. In the afternoons and evenings she settled down to her knitting, embroidery and mending; she also made tea and told me stories. Bottles of milk froze on the doorsteps, and Grandma used to put some frozen cream from the top of the bottle onto a saucer for me to eat. I liked making toast on a toasting fork in front of the open fire and listening to the radio.

Like many other villages, Ombersley didn't have mains water, sewerage or gas services. The winters were always the worst time for the elderly poor folk. They battled to keep their costs for food and heating to an absolute minimum, grimly determined to remain in their own homes however cold and damp they became. Many old cottages were very damp, roofs leaked, in some there was no electricity. Water was fetched from a hand pump or open well, turning the big handle to lower the bucket, then winding it back up when partly full, lifting it out and carrying it into the house. Old people who suffered from bronchitis became very poorly; every winter someone died of that or pneumonia, often referred to as *the old people's friend*. The cold, sometimes freezing winds, constant rainfall, frosty mornings and cold nights were part of the yearly cycle; in ours, and many households the amount of washing sharply decreased. Bed linen and clothing were only washed when absolutely necessary. Washing was dried indoors so living areas became steamy; often a clothes horse was placed in the living room in front of the fire, and steam and the odour of drying clothes filled the air. Small fires would be banked up with damp slack, beds were warmed with hot water bottles and had plenty of blankets on them with an eiderdown on top; people went to bed early to save fuel. There were always chamber pots under the beds to so that people didn't have to go outside to use the lavatory during the night.

THE COLLECTIVE WILL TO KEEP GOING

The steamy smell of unwashed clothing was not pleasant. We heard about a boy who rushed outside on a cold night to go to the lavatory down the garden. He tripped over in the dark, and fell into the "night soil" a place where the chamber pots and lavatory bucket contents had been buried! We laughed when we imagined the awful, filthy smelly state he must have been in, no doubt an unpleasant task for his mother when he returned to the house.

I was prone to tonsillitis, and had an operation to remove my tonsils and adenoids at a private nursing home when I was six years old. Unfortunately they screwed up the brace holding my mouth open for the operation so tightly that when the procedure was over my two, recently grown, second front teeth came out with this piece of equipment! To this day I can remember the pain when the brace was being tightened, even though I had been given a preoperative injection.

My family were horrified and legal action was threatened, following which I was referred to a Harley Street dental specialist (1943-48) who ran a monthly clinic in Birmingham. She moved all my top teeth by a slow process of bracing until the central gap had been filled and the teeth in that position were then crowned, "cutting edge" dentistry in those days! I continued to have bad coughs and colds every winter. I used up countless bottles of a cough mixture tasting and smelling strongly of garlic.

At our shop customers could obtain aspirins, a variety of cough mixtures and cough lozenges. My aunt and uncle made sure that the paraffin stoves were lit in the shop well before opening time, and burned all day at a low heat; customers were glad to come in and sit down for a chat when it wasn't busy. We all awoke to cold bedrooms with windows frosted with fascinatingly intricate icy patterns. We often had to wash in cold water, or wait until some had been heated on the stove. Homes were not insulated, doors and windows let in draughts, and heat from kitchens and living rooms was lost every time a door was opened because the rest of the home was usually cold. Some people hung thick curtains behind their outside doors in winter. Doors had to be closed as quickly as possible to keep out the freezing draught, which was difficult at the shop. The back door was opened frequently because access to the outside storage points was needed.

In those days religion seems to have been important to many people in communities such as ours; the Christian message was constantly reinforced. The size of our church congregation didn't vary, probably reflecting a group of people who adhered to the ways of their parents; for them the church calendar played an important part in the general pattern of life. They gave what they could afford to the collections and supported fund-raising events in any way they could. The church was where people were married, baptised their babies and buried their dead, whether they attended church regularly or not. The church provided some financial support to the poor and clergy visited the sick and dying when requested.

My father held no religious beliefs; Mother often disliked our Vicar's sermons after sitting through one in particular she decided to stop going to church. She joined the chapel congregation and I went to the chapel Sunday school for a while. This was short lived, Mum didn't like what the chapel offered; she stopped attending religious services and I went back to the church. Grandma never missed a Sunday service and my aunt and uncle sang in the choir. As a child I didn't understand arguments about hypocrisy, but it was a word I heard from time to time both in the shop and at home.

Shoe rationing began in 1943; civilians were limited to two pairs a year. The village cobbler, Mr. Sanders was kept busy repairing boots and shoes; shoes were made to last as long as possible. When children grew out of their boots and shoes, if there was any wear left in them they were handed on to others.

Clothing was rationed from June 1941; the Government's slogan was *Use it up, wear it out. Make it do, or do without*. Coupons allowed people to purchase one new outfit a year. A "War Production Board" was set up aiming to control the amount of fabric being used in clothing production. Women's skirts became shorter, pleats were minimal and zip fasteners disappeared because the metal was needed by the war ministry. Some children from poor families came to school in worn-out footwear and patched clothing. Mothers and grandmothers unravelled knitted garments, washed and rewound the yarn and knitted it up again into garments for the children.

The WI did the same, knitting socks, gloves and balaclavas for the troops. Coats were made from old blankets, the grey, khaki and dark blue ones which came from 25 MU Unit at Hartlebury were particularly sought after, and appeared from time to time. Ladies of the *Women's Institute* organised jumble sales, they also gave classes showing women how to use fabric from cast off clothing to make "new" clothes for children and themselves. Aunty Glad, who lived in Birmingham, bought lots of large balls of fine coloured string. She crocheted this, making lovely shopping bags that could be folded up easily to put into a handbag or pocket. She gave these away as presents and donated some to raise funds for her local church.

The fashion industry was challenged to produce new designs for clothes using less fabric; the results appealed to the young and newly emancipated women who had joined the forces, learned to drive and taken to wearing trousers. Older women wore lisle stockings held up with suspenders, and when holes appeared in these they mended them with needle and cotton. They also wore knee-length directoire knickers made in heavy cotton stockinette for winter and *Celanese* (a silky material) for warm weather. These garments had an elasticised waist and covered the upper legs to just above the knee where the hems were also elasticised. Some people called these knickers *passion killers* others referred to them as *apple scrumpers* because they were useful for carrying stolen fruit!

15

The older girls and young women had discovered short cami-knickers, which exposed most of the thigh area and showed suspenders and stocking tops when the skirt was lifted. For them nylon stockings came along with the American servicemen and were much in demand. Sometimes girls and young women coloured their skin to look tanned and used eyebrow pencil to draw a stocking seam up the backs of their legs. In the warm weather bare legs were *"in"*. Nylon stockings and nylon material could only be obtained on the "black market" as it was needed by the War Office for making parachutes. Children wore knee length socks in the winter months and ankle socks in the warmer months. In winter schoolgirls wore liberty bodices and thick, fleecy lined knickers with elastic threaded through the waist and leg hems. Boys remained in short trousers until they reached puberty; otherwise their clothing resembled that of their fathers. Families who were better off were easily identified, they were well dressed and had more extensive wardrobes. Those who were less well off had fewer clothes made of poorer quality material. Some *utility* clothing became shabby quickly, as the fabric was sub-standard and lacked durability.

Land Girls came to the village. Farmers were glad of help from the Women's Land Army which numbered more than 80,000 women in 1943. Typists, hairdressers, waitresses and mainly young women from other walks of life were keen to join up. They had a 50-hour working week and were given one week's paid holiday a year. I thought the ones who came to Ombersley looked very good in their green jerseys, brown jodhpurs and brown felt hats. They were trained to do all kinds of farm work; they could drive tractors and lorries, do the milking and help with the harvesting.

Some Land Girls quickly became disillusioned, however, as farm work in bad weather conditions, back-breaking weeding, clearing out ditches and hoeing work, muck-spreading and rat catching did not comply with the image the Government recruiting posters conjured up. These posters showed smiling Land Girls nursing lambs in a sunny rural scene. It is not surprising that some returned to their former employment.

But those who came to our village were hard-working girls who got along with everyone. They certainly did their bit towards the farming war effort.

The press and radio regularly reminded people how they should help the War Effort.

Private citizens and municipal authorities sacrificed their costly, beautifully designed gates and fences towards the vast amount of iron needed for the manufacture of tanks and ships. (We now know that a lot of that metal never reached the foundries, it was dumped in the Thames estuary.)

Collection points for scrap metal were set up, the Government encouraged salvage of as much aluminium as possible. People turned out disused and worn out pots and pans to be used for aircraft production.

Butchers saved all the bones they could. These were collected and used to make glue for aircraft production. Grandma used to ask the butcher for bones to make stock for soup and gravy.

I have heard that there was a scheme for salvaging horse chestnuts; in Ombersley there was always a large quantity of them from the church meadow trees which lined the main road and elsewhere in the village. It seems they were needed for use in the manufacture of explosives. However, none were salvaged in our village, the children continued to enjoy every conker season as usual.

Everyone had seen and heard the *Dig for Victory* slogan, but Ombersley villagers had always grown plenty of fruit and vegetables. Apples were carefully picked and stored for winter use; those with more fruit than they needed arranged for it to be collected so that it could be sent to market. The same applied to other fruits grown in gardens. The crops brought in a little money and nothing went to waste. The WI encouraged the making of preserves. Jellies, jams, chutneys and pickles were produced, some for home use, some to raise money for charitable causes. Sugar was rationed; the weekly amount of 12ozs. (340 grammes) per person had to be eked out in order to save some for this purpose. A few lucky villagers came by extra sugar if they knew someone who worked on the big river boats which transported it to Stourport-on-Severn. Workers were allowed to buy split sacks and spilt sugar that had been swept up. A good many sacks came along this way and the sugar was used for making homemade wine, cider and preserves.

Medicines and medical attention were expensive, the alternative was to consult someone who could prescribe herbal remedies. There were several people in

Ombersley who could do this, but villagers had learned many things from their parents and grandparents. Cabbage leaves were used to relieve wounds, onion juice and crushed parsley leaves were applied to insect bites. A poultice of boiled turnips was recommended for chilblains, raw potato was rubbed on chapped hands. For warts, the white juice from dandelion stems. The dandelion was also used in a tonic said to be good for the liver. Nettle "beer" was also a recommended tonic. The prolific hawthorn was used for many things, bark shavings were boiled and the liquid was given for insomnia and heart problems. In the Middle Ages it was used for the treatment of pleurisy and haemorrhaging. Cold tea was used to bathe eyes, and relieve scolds and burns.

A Jewish couple with a child came to live in the village soon after the war began. The little boy came to the village school and was made to stand outside the classroom during prayers and assemblies and was not allowed to attend any church services. The villagers adopted a rather cold, detached attitude towards them, Aunty Win said that other customers didn't seem very friendly towards them when they were in our shop. Many villagers never travelled further than around eighty miles of the village. Some hadn't been further than twelve miles from home, they seemed nervous of all foreigners.

Daddy had struck up a friendship with a coloured man at work and suggested bringing him home for a meal. Mum said this was definitely not a good idea, the family would object because customers would hear

19

about it. Gossip was almost a form of entertainment; there was always plenty for people to talk about. Sexual activities of the younger generations gave the old folk quite a lot to chew over. Eligible girls and lads flirted amongst themselves and extended their voyages of sexual discovery with interested parties from the older generation. There were several womanising men around who were well off with cars and wives at home. There were quite a few married women who discovered that marriage was not quite the safe haven they imagined.

Young women who remained unmarried after the age of 25 thought they were at risk of being "left on the shelf", that dreaded place occupied by old maids. Then the Yanks came along, the village Romeos had their noses put out of joint, they couldn't compete. However, none of the lovely young women were led up a leafy lane without previous explorations of the route!

CHAPTER
THREE

Life at School Bank

My parents set up home in this semi-detached house built in red brick, the first of six similar houses named "Coneygree Villas" which didn't seem to be quite in keeping with the rest of the village at that time. (The 14th century word "coney" means rabbit, the land was probably known as an area of rabbit warrens). These properties were owned by Mrs. Witherford who lived at No.6. Our house had three bedrooms, a box room, small hall, living room, kitchen, pantry and bathroom. It stood in quite a large garden, and had a brick built coal shed, attached to our only WC (it had a flush system but no hand basin). Heating came from coal fires or paraffin heaters; we did have an electric fire, a copper dish with a central cone-like element. Our living room was comfortably furnished, with enough space for a piano, two armchairs and a settee, and a big antique bureau standing in the bay window. On winter evenings we ate supper seated at the drop-leaf table in the middle of the room and relaxed around the fire reading or listening to the radio. My mother very often used the oil lamp to light the living room on long winter evenings to save money. Electricity was more expensive than oil or coal and she didn't want to get a big electricity bill. She worked in the family shop for four and a half days and earned about 50s per week; my father worked in the Government's MOD Maintenance Unit at Hartlebury during the war. Daddy's income was much lower than that his previous job in London. However the cost of living in Ombersley was less, they made ends meet and were glad to be there.

My parents worked hard, and their time at home was mostly spent working in or around the house. Daddy enjoyed gardening and grew lots of vegetables, he kept the grass on the two small lawns cut, and Mum helped to weed and hoe the flower beds. I can't say that they were happy all the time, I remember them bickering and being cross and disagreeable with each other. Mum always seemed glad when Daddy was asked to go as driver's mate on a big lorry to London and stay there for a night or two. She used to say things like "It's always better when we are on our own." Daddy was pleased to go too, he was able to visit his married sisters and brothers who lived in the East End.

Mum didn't take part in any of the village activities such as *WI*, and never went to the whist drives or dances. She listened to the radio and loved to read; she borrowed books from the library in Worcester; sometimes she went into Worcester with Grandma. She usually bought some fish and they had afternoon tea in *The White Tea Rooms* which was in Worcester's High Street in those days. She occasionally went to Kidderminster on the bus to have her hair waved; the hairdresser did that using hot curling irons.

Daddy enjoyed a bit of rough shooting from time to time, with his single barrelled .410 shotgun. I once went with him when he was intending to shoot pigeons in a coppice near to farmland where they were causing damage to crops; he carried his gun correctly broken with a pocket full of dark red cartridges. We saw plenty of pigeons, and Father used up his cartridges, but didn't manage to shoot one! We called to see a man who lived in the vicinity on our way home and Daddy bought a brace of pigeons to take home, telling me to keep that a secret; he wanted Mum to think he had shot them!

He occasionally played golf at Droitwich, but he never talked about it. I remember he looked very smart in his Harris Tweed plus-four suit, worn with diamond patterned long socks and splendid well-polished brogues. He carried his clubs in a canvas and leather golf bag that also contained his golfing shoes with spiked soles.

The kitchen was a focal point of day-to-day living. My earliest memories of this home focus particularly on time spent in the kitchen. It was furnished with a small table, three chairs and an armchair, which stood in front of the range. On the mantelpiece stood a wireless. We listened to the news and other programmes but the reception was not good and plenty of knob twiddling went on in efforts to get rid of the oscillation and interference. There was a clock by the radio and two china Staffordshire dogs stood on either end. Here and in all other ground floor rooms we had the same red tile flooring, which was polished with special red tile polish (another messy job) and there were rugs and mats in the living room, kitchen and hall. The kitchen mat and hearthrug had to be taken outside for shaking and brushing regularly. Above the kitchen sink was a window looking out onto the rear yard and garden. Our tabby cat named "Biddy" sat on the windowsill for hours watching the birds.

There was a built-in copper coal-fired boiler in the corner, which provided hot water for washing linen and clothes and for filling the bath. That sounds easy, but all the water had to be taken from the cold tap above the kitchen sink and poured into the boiler. The fire beneath the boiler had to be laid with kindling wood and coal and then there was quite a long wait until the water was hot enough to use. My mother huffed and puffed as she filled and emptied the boiler. Water was heated in this way and ladled into the sink to wash any clothing which couldn't be boiled. Wringing out each item as tightly as she could, she would drop them into a bucket, then go outside to use the small mangle to remove as much water as possible. The washing was hung on a washing line stretched across the small back yard area. In the winter the clothes would freeze when the weather was very cold and everything looked quite comical hanging stiffly, glistening and moving in the wind. It was not so funny for Mum; they would remain there until the temperature had risen and may possibly dry a little if the wind blew, or she may have to put them through the mangle again and bring it all into the kitchen to dry hanging over a clothes horse in front of the fire. The house filled with the smell of drying washing and steam on days like that. Once when I was getting dressed for school, Mum found that my clean vest was still damp, so she put it under her arm to air out a little more saying "Many a poor little mother has died from doing this for her children." My mother didn't enjoy washing or ironing; electric irons in those days were very basic with no temperature control, and steam irons hadn't been invented. Mother was pleased when "St. George's Laundry" of Worcester started a round to our village. She saved up money to send the sheets and large towels to the laundry, in the van that called once a fortnight.

There was quite a large pantry next to the kitchen; it contained wooden shelves, a cold stone slab and a meat safe stood below the window. The meat/food safe was a small wooden cupboard with one shelf inside, well ventilated by metal mesh panels to keep out flies and insects. A blue enamel bread bin with BREAD in white letters on one side stood on the cold shelf. Underneath was a large open-topped stoneware bowl in which eggs were kept in a solution of isinglass to preserve them for winter use. This was a very satisfactory way of keeping fresh eggs for use when they were not so plentiful. The isinglass (a gelatine or glue made from fish viscera) acted as a sealing agent to the porous egg shells; eggs preserved in this way could be used in the same ways as fresh eggs, it was however necessary to pierce the shells at either end with a pin or needle before boiling them. The shelves which ran along two walls of the pantry were used for food storage. On them were a couple of roughly constructed racks made from old orange boxes fixed together and standing on end, which were used to store green tomatoes picked at the end of the season and placed on newspaper to ripen, cooking apples, and vegetables from the garden. The eating apples were wrapped in newspaper and lasted well into the winter months, especially the "Russet" apples. The ironing board and brooms were kept there too.

We had a tabby cat named Biddy who produced two litters of four kittens every year, only mating with the same old big scruffy tabby who always appeared when she was in season. Mother drowned all the kittens before they opened their eyes, taking them out of Biddy's box by the range when she was outside and put them in the coal-shed. Then, after dark she put on some rubber gloves and took a bucket of water into the coal-shed where she held each kitten under until it was dead, without looking! She wrapped the tiny corpses in newspaper and put them in the dustbin. Biddy lived until she was about nine years old, and must have had 80 kittens in all. We kept one from her final litter. (We called him James and he lived until 1960.)

I shall always remember "Biddy" bringing in tiny rabbits she had caught; she carried them by the scruff of their necks, and always placed them carefully under the piano. Sometimes in the summer we would hear a noise from that direction and became accustomed to fishing out a baby rabbit. We took them back up the garden to the long grass by the hedge on the other side of our fence in the hope that their mothers would find them. There was plenty of evidence of the continuing rabbit habitat. When Mum went to Worcester she brought back some fish heads to boil up for cat food.

In their early days at School Bank, all cooking was done on the cast iron coal-fired range which had to be "black-leaded" regularly to keep it clean. This was a filthy job. Mother had to rub plenty of black-lead polish all over the ironwork then brush it off with a soft brush until it shone. All the ash had to be emptied out first, and the ovens had to be brushed out too. She didn't have any protective gloves and her hands became ingrained with the black of the polish, a filthy job. It was a big event when a second-hand electric cooker was purchased and installed by the village electrician. It had three hotplates and an oven, such an innovation, but we did miss the fire and warmth of the old range. Later another "modern" appliance was purchased, a *Belling* tabletop electric grill with a hot plate on the top; that was a real luxury — it made cooking breakfasts and quick meals much easier. It had a hotplate on top on which the frying pan was used, and the grillpan slid underneath to grill bacon, tomatoes and sausages — when we had them. Mum didn't enjoy cooking, so meals were very plain and ordinary, depending on what was available from the garden, what could be obtained with our food ration coupons and what she could afford.

My parents were finding country life very different. The plumbing at our house was very basic, but many of the cottages and houses in areas surrounding our village had neither running water nor mains drainage. Our mirror-less bathroom lead off the kitchen, and in there was only an enamel bath with no water supply; but the bathwater could be drained away when the plug was taken out. A small table covered with a cloth stood by the bath, and on it stood a flowered china washbasin with matching jug. A freestanding wooden towel rail was beneath a small shelf used for the oil lamp and candlestick. There was no electric light in the bathroom, although the small window above the bath gave light in summer time. On bath nights the boiler was lit, filled with water from the kitchen tap and then ladled back into the bucket when hot and tipped into the bath. Bath water was shared, me first (when I was too old to be bathed in an enamel hip bath in front of the fire), then Mum followed by Dad. Other families living in similar houses managed in the same way, adding more hot water as required until all the family had finished their ablutions. Daddy always shaved in front of a mirror hanging near to the kitchen sink. He used to sharpen his razor on a long leather strap which hung from a hook behind the kitchen door. The unheated bedrooms were certainly chilly in winter time; we all awoke to find our windows frosted over with fascinating patterns on the inside of the glass on cold mornings. At night Mother put hot water bottles in the beds to warm them, and I had a blanket sleeping bag in my bed.

I was not always a good child in those days. We went to Worcester one day when I was about six years old to buy me some new shoes. We caught the bus, and went to "Elt's", the main shoe shop where they had an X-ray machine through which you could see if the shoes fitted the feet correctly. I was very pleased with the brown leather bar strap shoes and carried the box wrapped in brown paper and tied with string, until we returned home. Then I opened the package and tried on my new shoes again, asking if I could wear them until bedtime. Mum said "No." I was upset about this, so I argued, shouted and stamped my feet. Mother again said "No", adding, "You are a naughty girl, you just don't realise what I gave up to have you!" I replied "Well, I didn't ask to be born!" I was quickly put to bed with a smack and lights out.

My bedroom was small; I kept some of my books and toys there, but I also had a shelf for my things in the large cupboard by the chimney breast in the living room. When I went to bed, I had to kneel by my bed and say my prayers every night before the light was put out:

Gentle Jesus meek and mild,
Look upon this little child,
God bless Mummy and God bless Daddy and
Make me a good girl. Amen.

Sometimes Mum read me a story, sometimes the room was too cold, so I had to snuggle down and go to sleep with my feet on the hot-water bottle. When I had learned to read, I was allowed to read to myself for a while before the light was switched off. Once I had become a really fluent reader, I used to continue reading under the bedclothes using a torch!

CHAPTER
FOUR

Life at "The Shop"

My other home was at *Pester's Stores* in the centre of Ombersley village. My grandparents Annie and John Pester lived there. Grandpa was a genial man (born in 1870) who had taken his doctor's advice and retired from his busy life in West Bromwich. He was told to take plenty of rest, and it seemed life in a country village would be the answer; they arrived in Ombersley in 1936. Aunty Win lived with them and worked in the shop. Grandma helped, then when my mother arrived she worked in the shop too. When I was about five years old Aunty Win married and her husband, John Smith, lived at the shop too.

Grandpa enjoyed going to *The King's Arms* for a drink or two at midday, as he had made friends with several men whose company he enjoyed. No doubt he regaled them with stories of his experiences at country markets and amongst the townsfolk in West Bromwich. He usually wore a tweed suit with a waistcoat and most of his shirts had separate starched collars, around which he always wore a silk tie. He liked his beer and whisky and was interested in horseracing, and often put on a small bet if he fancied a particular horse.

Grandma told me that one year he kept a record of all his bets and winnings; he broke even with his bookmaker at the end of the year and was pleased about that.

He had a pair of gold pocket watches attached to a gold chain; these were carried in his waistcoat pockets with the chain safely secured in a buttonhole, and a gold seal dangling from the chain. He used to sink into his big leather armchair in the dining room and sit me on his knee when he came home from the pub. Then he would take out both his watches and hold them to my ears so that I could hear them ticking. I was always fascinated when he opened the backs of the watches so I could see the intricate movements at work.

He was a kindly old gent who had known a hard working life. When I climbed down from his lap he would pick up the newspaper and read for a few minutes; when I peeped round the door I always found him snoring contentedly with his silk handkerchief over his face moving with rhythmical regularity. Sadly, Grandpa's retirement didn't last very long he passed away in 1940 while I was still an infant.

Grandma often held me in her arms when I was little, as she looked after me while my Mum worked in the shop. Mum thought this would be a good idea, and when the weather was warm enough for us to sit outside she obtained a playpen to put on the lawn, so that I could play in it safely with Grandma in her chair. I vociferously let them know that this plan did not suit me! I wanted to be on the move and toddle around freely, so Mum put me in the pram and took me for a walk until I went to sleep.

As I grew older I spent so much of my time with Grandma. She cooked for the family, and I stood or sat by the big table in the kitchen behind the shop helping her to prepare meals or make puddings, cakes and pastry. I was allowed to help, and learned a great deal that way. We talked all the time. Gran's kitchen was always a busy place. Every morning at eleven o'clock she made up a tray with mugs of hot drinks and a plate of cake or pastries, to take into the shop for their break. Aunty Win and her husband John ran the shop; he drove the van, attended to the garden and exercised the two spaniel dogs.

One day when I was on holiday from school, Grandma said she was going to Allington's farm, because Mrs. Allington wanted to learn how to make butter, and I went with her. It was a warm summer's day and we talked as we walked down the main road turning into Sinton Lane and then passing the black and white cottages until we came to the farmhouse. Mrs. Allington came to the kitchen door and took us into the dairy where she showed Grandma the churn she had acquired. It was an old 19th century wooden end-over-end churn, which Gran said was just like those she had used at home and at her brother's farm in Abberley.

Gran put on her apron, and checked the temperature in the dairy, commenting that 55°F to 60°F was just right. She removed the lid from the top of the churn barrel, looked inside, asked if the churn had been properly scalded and cleaned, inspected it and was satisfied. Mrs. Allington showed her the cream she had ready, they put it into the churn, fastened the lid in place and Grandma began turning the handle. To me, it seemed an absolute age before the sound of the cream inside changed indicating that it had formed a fairly solid ball, which we could see through the peep hole. It had probably taken about fifteen minutes of steady churning to reach this point. Grandma placed a bowl beneath the churn to catch the whey when she removed the bung from the drainage hole. Then the lid was removed and she tipped the churn so that the ball of butter could fall into another large bowl. She asked for a jug of cold water and poured some over the butter, then she kneaded it until the buttermilk was extracted, adding a little salt and working it well in.

Mrs. Allington brought some small pudding basins, the butter was pressed into the basins, and covered with cold water. Gran said the butter should keep for ten to twelve days like that in a cool larder or cellar, providing the water was tipped out and replaced every day. I really enjoyed that afternoon, and told my friends all about it.

Grandma enjoyed knitting, and could knit men's socks on four needles, expertly turning the heels and finishing off the tops with neat ribbing. She was good at embroidery too, and made lovely tablecloths. Ironing and mending were her jobs too; in those days socks were darned using a wooden "mushroom" and sheets worn in the middle were turned sides to middle so that maximum use was made of them. Grandma often turned the sheets, stitching the long seams by hand — a run and fell seam down the centre and ordinary hemming at the sides. She had a sewing machine, but preferred to sit and hand-sew that way she could listen to *Mrs. Dale's Diary* on the wireless; sometimes she listened to *Children's Hour* with me.

THE KITCHEN

The kitchen was an oblong room in which the large wooden scrubbed-top table was a main feature on the wall opposite the sink. On this sturdy table Grandma prepared meals for the family. Her tools were in drawers beneath the tabletop. Three old wooden chairs and two stools beside it. Wearing her large apron, she stood at the end of the table preparing endless vegetables. I was taught *below the ground (root) vegetables go into cold water*, and *above the ground (green) vegetables should have boiling water*. I was growing up and taking an interest in cooking; I loved making pastry and cakes.

We talked as she worked, making pastry, pies, puddings and a range of meat dishes and I was allowed to help with some things. In school holidays, I remember learning the names of the herbs in the garden and being shown how to pick, clean and prepare them. I washed fruit and stirred jam, then stuck the labels on the jars. I was fascinated watching Grandma skin and dress hares and rabbits. She plucked and dressed all kinds of poultry and game and could expertly clean and bone all types of fish. There was an electric cooker in the kitchen. Gran cooked breakfast, lunch and the evening meal and I helped Aunty Win with the washing up. They closed the shop at lunch times and Mum went home to prepare an evening meal or do a bit of housework, returning to work behind the counter again on four afternoons each week.

THE PRIVY

There were four doors in the kitchen, one was the back door opening onto the garden path, and one was a door to what my family called *the privy room*. This small boarded room contained a large white porcelain lavatory with a heavy hinged wooden seat. Above it was the patterned cast iron cistern with a chain and a blue and white ceramic handle on the end to operate the flush. The privy also had wall hooks for hanging coats, overalls etc., and a cupboard for shoes, with a basket of shoe-cleaning materials on top. There were shelves on the walls where vases, washing powder and cleaning materials were kept. A green wooden box containing furniture polish, silver and brass polish and a basket of dusters and rags stood on another shelf, and the mop and bucket lived in there too. The picture wouldn't be complete without the hats, dogs' leads, brooms and wellingtons.

THE MORNING ROOM

A door between the privy room and the kitchen sink led into the Morning Room, which was a family room where meals were taken on a dining table large enough for eight people when extended. Here there was a "Triplex" fireplace with two ovens constantly in use in the cold weather. The "Triplex" was considered very modern; it had a cream and light brown enamel exterior, very easy to clean. I loved that room and used to sit in the big armchair by the fire to listen to *Children's Hour* on the wireless when I came home from school. The window looked out onto the lawn and garden.

LUCY DID THE WASHING

Lucy was a strong, energetic person whom the family valued. Her hair was always tied up in a scarf tied at the front, allowing a dark straggly fringe to fall over her forehead. She had thick eyebrows above deep-set brown eyes; her nose always seemed red, as she had a constant cold which made her frequently sniff loudly, and her mouth hung open. Lucy always seemed to wear a wrap-around apron covering her ample bosom. Her legs were sturdy and her ankles thick above wide loose-fitting shoes. In the winter she wore ankle socks over her lisle stockings, or fur-lined boots with a zip up the front. She wore short-sleeved blouses or jumpers for work. Lucy spoke with a broad Worcestershire country accent, dropping all her aitches and softly rolling her "r"s. She lived in an old cottage close to the woodland at the end of Church Lane and worked three mornings a week for Grandma. On Mondays she got stuck into the heavy household washing, using the coal-fired copper boiler in the corner of the kitchen before they bought an electric boiler.

Washdays were steamy, and the outside door had to be kept open. The boiler was filled with water from the sink, then soap powder and soda crystals were added. The sheets, pillow-cases, towels, tea towels and table cloths were boiled first. When they had been boiled for long enough they were lifted out with wooden tongs, dropped into a bucket and transferred to the deep ceramic sink for rinsing and hand-wringing. I thought it was funny when I saw her wipe her running nose on the back of her wet hand and carry on rinsing or wringing! A blue-bag was added to the rinsing water to enhance the colour of the whites. The remaining soapy water in the boiler was used to wash soiled working clothes, dusters etc. before the boiler was emptied.

When Lucy had rinsed and hand-wrung out the first batch, she took it all outside and put it through the big mangle standing near to the back door. Then she carried the washing in a big basket to the washing line behind a tall hedge in the back garden; the hedge had been planted so that washing couldn't be seen from the living rooms. Lucy did the handwashing next, using a bar of green washing soap to rub stained parts of clothing and sometimes a washboard or a small brush.

The kitchen floor was pretty wet on washdays and Lucy's hands became red and chapped in the winter. I remember Grandma telling her to rub her hands with slices of raw potato to ease her chaps and chilblains.

THE HALL AND DINING ROOM

The front door to the house from the village street led up a short passage into a wider hallway area; from there doors led into the dining room, sitting room, cellar, shop, morning room and garden. Visitors came in that way and left their coats and hats in the hall. There was a big chair by the grandfather clock. At Christmas time, people who sang in the church choir with Aunty Win and Uncle John came in to have a drink after the morning service. Aunty Win would play the piano in the sitting room, and with voices lubricated by sherry etc. more carols were sung. Tommy Styles was Headmaster, often among the people who came in, he enjoyed a glass or two!

The dining room was furnished with a big dark oak table and eight high-backed chairs with green velvet seats. It was a good room for family parties; the big fireplace had a wide chimney and the fires burned well. The tall, heavily carved sideboard held a collection of silver-plated entrée dishes; the large oval one with a hinged lid was a chafing dish, the cut glass cruet had a silver-plated stand and handle, as did the pair of decanters. Grandma was proud of her bits of silver plate and Lucy used to keep them well polished. The room looked lovely at Christmas time when the holly was behind the pictures, the fire burning and the table laid with a starched white cloth and all the plates, cutlery and Christmas Crackers. One Christmas, the crackers formed the skirt of a crinoline dress on a doll. We had memorable family parties with plenty of laughter and singing. However, when there were too many women in the kitchen, tempers became frayed and sharp words were said!

THE CELLAR

The cellar had ancient stone walls and it was always cold down there. There was a huge central stone slab "table" providing useful storage space for the butter, lard, margarine and perishable foodstuffs sold in the shop. A wide stone topped shelf ran along the walls with spaces beneath for wine storage. We had no refrigerator, so Grandma used the cellar to keep food fresh for the family. Her preserves were also kept in this cool, dark space.

CHILLY BEDROOMS

Upstairs were five bedrooms and a bathroom with hot and cold water, a flush toilet, and a washbasin with taps and a mirror above. There was an airing cupboard in there too with an immersion heater in it. The bathroom was large enough to house a big cupboard with carved doors, which provided shelf space for bed linen and towels. To get to Grandma's bedroom over the morning room, you had to walk through the bathroom; I remember a funny little staircase between the morning room and that bedroom being removed to give more space to the bedroom. None of the bedrooms had any form of heating and if the weather was very cold Grandma had an electric fire in hers to warm it up. But the frost would be on the inside of the windows in the windows in the mornings, just like everyone else's.

I had a little bedroom at the back of the property on the left at the top of the stairs. It had a funny window very high up in the wall, in fact the wall opposite the bedroom door adjoined Morris's property (now the *Venture Inn*). I loved that small room and used to lie in bed at night listening to the mice playing in the roof space above the ceiling. Grandma always came to tuck me in and sometimes sat on my bed to read me a poem or a short story from one of my books, which were kept on a small chest of drawers. I also had a wooden Noah's Ark made for me by Uncle John, that had some small animals inside which my Daddy bought from a toy shop in Broad Street in Worcester. That stood on the chest of drawers by my hairbrush and comb. There was a tall narrow cupboard for hanging clothes, with a drawer underneath where I kept some of my toys and things. "Bruin", my big brown bear, lived on the bed and I had a little basket of sewing things there too. I loved that room, and was always very happy to go to bed there, especially if I had had a lovely hot bath and was sipping "Ovaltine" or "Milo" from a mug while Gran sat on my bed.

CHAPTER
FIVE

Our Shop

The English are often referred to as "A Nation of Shopkeepers", and my family were certainly among them. Our shop was located in the centre of Ombersley village, the sign above the door was J.W. Pester — General Stores. John William Pester, my Grandfather leased the property from Ombersley Church Houses Charity around 1935. He and my grandmother, moved to Ombersley following his retirement from family owned businesses in West Bromwich. There he had learned about shopkeeping from his father and uncles. He and his brothers had fruit and vegetable shops in Lower Queen Street and Bull Street; and their fish shop and a large fruit and vegetable shop was located at 214-216 High Street, West Bromwich. Grandma and Grandpa began their married life in a house at the back of these shops, their children were born there and they both worked very hard.

The Ombersley shop was formerly a newsagents' also selling cigarettes, tobacco and a limited range of food items in the shop area. There was a tearoom on the premises too, which was set up in the room on the left of the front door to the house. (This part of the property is considerably older than the rest, 13th-14th century, originally called *The Priest's House*.) In fine weather teas were served outside in the rear garden. The rest of the property is a 15th century building heavily plastered over, covering all the old wooden structure — probably originally owned by Evesham Abbey. The shop itself has had the same frontage for a very long time, the door flanked by bay windows on either side; the front of the house was on the left, comprising another door and window.

The shop door opened close to a counter on the left; a glass display fitting for tobacco and cigarettes stood upon it, followed by a lower glass fitting displaying wrapped sweets and chocolate bars. On top of that stood a row of large glass jars containing many kinds of boiled sweets. Loose sweets were served onto small scales, then tipped into paper bags: the big cash till took up the remaining space on that counter.

Along the right hand side of the shop ran a long counter, and the walls on both sides of the shop were lined with wooden shelving from floor to ceiling. At the rear of the shop on the left wall the shelving contained many small polished wooden-fronted drawers where spices and seasonings were stored. Halfway along the shop floor space a large counter was stacked with biscuit tins, on the left of those stood the majestic red bacon slicing machine, and on the right were large scales. Customers could not go past that point. The staff worked behind the counters and at the back of the shop where the cutting and weighing up was done. There were a couple of steps up to two doors at the back of the shop; the one in the middle led into the kitchen and the other, in the left corner, opened into the house hallway adjacent to the big cellar door.

In the early days they used to employ an errand boy, named Hesketh (Frank?) who lived in Hay Lane; he rode the large black delivery bicycle with a big basket over the front wheel.

The shop was closed on Thursday afternoons and when Aunty Win and Uncle John drove into Worcester to go to the wholesalers. Uncle John always drove the van, as my Aunt had never learned to drive. Uncle John did the grocery deliveries to customers who lived outside the village on Fridays and Saturdays. They employed a young lady called Gwen Green to serve in the shop, who I think was there on the busy days — Wednesdays, Fridays and Saturdays.

Rationing was in force and our registered customers had official Ration Books containing food coupons. Every household had to register with a shop, and in 1940 the rations of bacon and butter were 4oz. (115g.) per person per week, 12oz. (340g.) sugar per person per week and in 1941 1oz. (30g.) cheese per person per week. In 1940 meat was rationed to approximately 1lb. (450g) per person per week, in practice more was available for those prepared to take the cheaper cuts. There was always "Spam" tinned meat and plenty of recipes for using it. Supplies of eggs, and canned and fresh milk were allocated to shops and suppliers according to numbers of registered customers. The official egg ration was 1 egg per person per fortnight; supplies were not guaranteed, so in towns and cities people had to fall back on the Government's dried egg substitute. In the country people kept chickens and usually had enough eggs for their own use and to swap for coupons for other foodstuffs; swapping of coupons was common, a sensible way of sharing supplies. There was a points system for cereals, biscuits, canned meat, fruit and fish; these were often "under the counter" because of limited supply. Customers got used to saying "Anything UTC?" (Anything under the counter?) A policy of fair shares for all was maintained.

My grandfather had made contracts with biscuit manufacturers, soap merchants and with Messrs. Marsh & Baxters for bacon and ham. These goods were supplied to our shop at the agreed quantities throughout the war years. Other supplies of dried fruit, condiments, cheese, butter, margarine and lard were ordered and delivered from the wholesale merchants in Worcester. There were other wholesalers who specialised in cigarettes, tobacco, confectionery and luxury goods. Aunty Win used to buy things like cosmetics, toiletries, first-aid requirements and proprietary medicines from them, for which she paid cash, and brought them back in the van.

SERVING THE CUSTOMERS

As soon as a customer came in and said they wanted several items, a ruled receipt book was placed on the counter and the person serving wrote down the item and price as they were placed on the counter. Most of our customers came into the shop with a bag or basket and tended to sit on one of the three chairs, especially if they had walked from a distance away. They placed their ration books on the counter and asked for each item required. Serving a customer with a list of items meant a lot of running around the shop gathering things from shelves all around the walls and taking them back to the counter, even though everything was located in a logical way. A lot of weighing up had to be done, large whole cheeses had to be cut through with a wire and then cut again to smaller pieces according to the weight required. Weighed pieces of cheese were wrapped in greaseproof paper, put in a paper bag and taken to the customer. For some time butter, margarine and lard also came in large blocks, which was also cut and wrapped by hand. Fortunately flour and sugar came in packets, but biscuits were delivered to us in 12lb. tins. Customers requiring half a pound of one type and half a pound of another type had their requirements separately weighed and bagged up. Many other items were stocked and served in this labour intensive manner.

Uncle John usually cut the bacon on the big shiny red bacon slicing machine; it ran so smoothly as the handle was turned and sliced the bacon perfectly to the exact thickness preferred by the customer. The sides of smoked and plain bacon were hung in a large meat "safe" (a wooden framed cupboard with pierced metal (rather like strong metal lace) panels on all sides, at the back of the shop. When there was more bacon than would fit into the "safe", it was hung in the cellar. Sometimes I watched Uncle John cut and bone out the bacon sides (scraping out maggots from beneath the bones when necessary).

STORAGE OF STOCK WAS COMPLICATED

Our dining room was just across the hall from the door into the shop, and at times the big table in there was covered with cardboard boxes of chocolate bars and other confectionery items. This didn't cause any problems with family life because the morning room had an extending dining table and chairs where we ate most of our meals, and the dining room was only used for special occasions. A large spare bedroom was used to store the big cartons of cereals and washing powder. An outside storeroom, referred to as "the engine room", housed the wooden boxes of unwrapped white toilet soap, green washing soap, abrasive soap (for deeply grimed hands), and red carbolic soap. I was always fascinated with the old wooden knife-sharpening machine with a big handle on one side and many slots for knives in several sizes kept in there. A stag's head with great antlers hung on the wall, which had a certain wild, glassy-eyed expression. I used to wonder where it had come from and tried to imagine the size of the whole animal and the scene of its death.

The walled rear garden behind our shop had a good sized lawn area, flower borders, a rockery and rose arches over the pathways leading to the buildings at the far end. These were originally screened off by a hedge of lilac, but that was replaced with a privet hedge. It was always a pretty garden; peonies, dahlias, Michaelmas daisies, and other perennial herbaceous plants provided plenty of colour. A great pear tree stood on the left and a damson tree was in the right-hand side of the lawn. The outbuildings afforded plenty of space; on the left-hand end of the largest, chickens were kept, nesting boxes stood against the wall and there were roosting poles across the central space. The floor was scattered with sawdust and there was a ventilated door leading to the adjoining wire-fenced pen where the hens scratched around during the day. A central room was used for storing the lawn mower and garden equipment; another storeroom at the end of the main part was used for coal and the big paraffin tank. A tanker came at regular intervals during the winter months to refill the tank. Customers brought their oilcans to the shop and when Uncle John was around he went up the garden path to fill them. The whole of that building had loft space above, the loft door being in the wall above the door to the coal and paraffin store. Another building at the back of the garden had a loft with an external wooden staircase leading to it which Uncle John used as his carpentry workshop. Their golden cocker spaniel dog called "Goldy" was once kept in there when she had a litter of puppies. The room below was used for firewood and storing all the empty biscuit tins.

I hope this has given you a picture of our shop; it is continued in *Comings and Goings*, where I describe some of the interaction with customers.

CHAPTER
SIX

Comings and Goings

The short days, frosty mornings and cold winds of winter brought folks into our shop closing the door with relief. Sometimes they went to the black paraffin stove to warm their hands and get their breath back if they had been walking against the wind. When winter set in the demand for paraffin increased considerably Uncle John, Aunty Win, Gwen and my mother did a lot of traipsing up and down the garden path to fill paraffin cans. Uncle John kept the brick pathway salted on frosty mornings and after clearing snow away. Raincoats were kept near the back door.

There was often laughter in the shop as anecdotes were exchanged and accounts of amusing mishaps or misunderstandings were told. There were very few secrets in our village, everyone knew everyone else, any change in routine or unusual occurrence was immediately noticed and commented upon. Word spread around the village at an amazing speed. My family found the "village telegraph" both valuable and annoying. People in need of help found offers from friends and neighbours came very quickly; people expressed empathy, sympathy and practical help.

Accounts of family quarrels, disputes with neighbours, affairs of the heart, financial difficulties and sporting misadventures of all kinds spread like wildfire, often gaining embellishments on the way like "Chinese whispers"! My family were amused and interested in talking to the customers but tried to keep a tactful distance, refraining from expressing opinions. Sometimes people criticised others in a very cruel way; jealousy regularly reared its ugly head. My family also had disagreements, sometimes heated ones. My mother and Aunty Win were always jealous of their sister, my Aunty Glad who lived in Birmingham, married to a man with money and a very good job. They were all people who had strongly held opinions about a lot of things. At the shop they were sometimes irritable and short tempered behind the scenes; it seemed to me that each one wanted to be "boss" because they knew better, but they kept it away from the public eye and ear.

One old fellow named Dan who worked on the land came in for his usual tobacco and asked my uncle for a tin of mustard. Uncle John said, "What d'you want that for Dan, isn't the 'baccy strong enough?" Dan laughed and said "Me baccy is as good as ever, but I can't eat the missus's bricks uv out mustard!" Dan's wife made pies from fresh meat trimmings she asked the butcher to save. She didn't care what mixture of meats they were and sometimes she added breadcrumbs to make the meat go further. She always asked for some free bones to boil up and make the strong stock, which set like jelly in the pies. The crust was thick raised pastry; when baked it became brown and very hard. Dan ate

49

these "bricks" for his lunch when he was working in the fields.

The majority of villagers didn't have a telephone. Sometimes the milkman's wife came in with a list of things wanted by someone who was unwell and couldn't get to the shop; her husband would deliver the shopping with the milk the next day. The milkman would also call at the doctor's surgery occasionally to request a visit if someone needed the doctor.

We had a customer who I will call Maud, whose large family lived in a broken down cottage along one of the lanes. The father of her schoolaged children was killed at the beginning of the war, but Maud kept going and gave birth to two more children, probably by different fathers. It was said in a meaningful way that she associated with the Italian and Polish prisoners of war from a camp near Droitwich who came to work on farms nearby. Her older children did some farm work after school and in the holidays when they were needed. Maud worked as a cleaner and general help for people with a large house. She was a big woman and her good nature and sense of humour radiated from her beaming face. She didn't give a toss about village gossip, each new addition to her family was loved and cared for even if their home was brim full. One of her elder girls could play the piano. She couldn't read music and was self-taught, but she could thump out all the latest songs. There was often this kind of music and happy voices singing the words of popular songs of the day — *It's a long way to Tipperary, The White Cliffs of Dover, I'm looking over a four leafed clover, She'll be coming round the mountain* etc. Maud had the gift of making people laugh; everyone was smiling when she had been in the shop.

Mrs. Marsh was an important person around the village; she was the widow of the man who founded the "Marsh and Baxter" pork butchery company in Birmingham. She lived in a large mansion house in one of the "Hamptons", a group of hamlets between Ombersley and Hartlebury. Occasionally she drove herself into the village in her large shining car, always wearing a smart hat. Her appearances usually caused comments from those who saw her; people often found something derogatory to say. She had worked hard to help her husband with his business and was trying to modify her "Brummie" accent. I recall that she had quite a loud voice and said, "Aave you any . . . ?" emphasising the "a"s and dropping the "h". She sometimes ordered provisions by telephone, which made my mother laugh if she took the call. Uncle John delivered her orders once a week and at other times if she was "Aaving a bit of a doo."

Occasionally commercial travellers drove up and parked outside the door. One came in and introduced himself saying he wanted to show us a new, exciting product named "Smith's Potato Crisps". He placed packets of crisps on the counter and invited my mother, aunt and uncle to taste them; they were *not* particularly enthusiastic. He said his company had just put them on the market and they seemed to be selling quite well. They may have ordered a small quantity, as it would have been something people could buy without using coupons. The representative then said he could also offer them the opportunity to buy shares in "Smiths Crisps" company, but they declined the offer saying they didn't think potato crisps would catch on!

I remember once hearing Aunty Win and my mother discussing the assistant, Gwen, saying that they would have to watch her very carefully when she was serving her relatives. They were worried in case she undercharged them or didn't charge for some items in an order or when they came to the counter. Gwen was a very nice young woman, always smartly dressed, polite and cheerful. I liked her very much and she certainly worked hard.

Of course we had moaners and groaners; one woman called Betty *always* seemed to have a cold; she sniffled, blew her nose and sometimes made a noise at the back of her throat as she tried to loosen the catarrh. Betty never seemed to be happy, she complained about the weather, her chilblains in winter, her dislike of hot weather and her various aches and pains; she was never without something to moan about. She hated washing and always told people exactly how many items she had washed by hand and hung out on the line. Another customer once asked her how many pegs she had used!

Betty complained about the food rationing and not being able to get things she wanted. When she bought biscuits she always said, "Don't get putting any broken ones in *my* bag." Her bacon had to be cut to No.5 thickness and she complained if there was a bit of extra rind or if it seemed more salty than usual. She was a practiced grumbler, adding her comments to any subject raised; she could go on and on about items from the radio news. When doors and windows were open in summertime, she objected to hearing music from a neighbour's radio. She constantly criticised her neighbours and seemed unable to find anything to smile about.

When I came home from school on Friday afternoons our shop was always very busy, sometimes filled with people. Mum was always very tired on Friday evenings, and sometimes I went home with her and we had a meal with Daddy and then listened to the wireless. Sometimes I stayed at the shop and spent the evening with Gran, Aunty Win and Uncle John. I always enjoyed having a bath there. Gran ran the water and got out a big towel for me, and the bathroom was always warm.

There was a constant stream of people coming into the shop on Saturdays too. Children came in to spend pocket money buying sweets; they always had their sweet coupons with them, and tended to buy inexpensive things like *sherbet suckers* (small paper packets containing white fizzy sherbet powder with a straw to suck it through) and twisted barley sugar sticks. Bull's eyes were popular because they lasted a long time and changed colour as they were sucked.

At Christmas time Aunty Win always put out a small display of fancy gift items; the men who came in for their cigarettes and tobacco appreciated that. When they had been paid, they bought gifts for their families. The centre counter was trimmed with brightly coloured paper and a display of fancy tins of talcum powder, bottles of eau de cologne, jars of face-cream, boxes of soap, manicure sets, hand-cream etc. was arranged. One year we had a row of boxed Christmas crackers at the back of all those small items. Not everyone had the time or money to go to the big stores in Worcester or Kidderminster, so they were pleased to find these things at our shop.

The shop was always a place where people talked and laughed. The family were ready to listen to folk with problems and to those who were feeling down for some reason. The customers talked to each other and the repartee was spontaneous and often very funny; it all seems very quaint as I describe it, but it served the community and had its day.

CHAPTER
SEVEN

Home Deliveries

In the early days, the family employed young Hesketh to do small deliveries on the bicycle with a large basket over the front wheel. Uncle John delivered to outlying places in the small van. My mother, her sister and Gwen packed the orders in cardboard boxes. As they did this they followed the customer's handwritten order list (they used to have many a laugh at the spelling errors!). The name and cost of each item was entered on the bill, also making a carbon copy. When the orders had been assembled, Aunty Win checked the total for each order written clearly on the bottom of the list. Food ration books were in use and coupons had to be used for many food items. These were sometimes handed in with the order or had to be collected when it was delivered.

I used to rush home from the village school on Fridays to go out in the van and help my uncle with the deliveries. Most of the people we delivered to had no means of transport other than bicycles. I liked calling at the homes of people who worked on the land, as they always had a cheery word. There was one family with lots of children, where they allowed the chickens to run in and out of the cottage, and kept a goat in the garden. The children were never particularly clean or well dressed, but they were always laughing and playing with each other. Another family had cherry trees in a small orchard at the back of their cottage, and when the fruit was ripe the lady often offered me a glass of cherry juice. Although the few better off villagers had cars, they too expected their goods to be delivered. My uncle didn't collect money from them, payment was made by cheque or cash when they called at the shop. I used to love driving down the lane past The Ripperidge Inn to call at Major Colville's farm. He was always so cheerful and talkative and sometimes he came out and took the box from my uncle and paid the bill there and then.

We delivered weekly groceries to an old man who lived in a cottage in Sytchampton, and had a huge old tabby tom-cat who was particularly partial to humbugs! Naturally humbugs were always on his order, and I was fascinated to see the cat take one from him and chew it, the spittle running from the sides of its mouth as it sat there on the doorstep.

In the school holidays I sometimes went to stay with Aunty Glad in Birmingham. She used to take me on the bus into the centre of the city, and we would go to a shop called "Barrows", where she placed her grocery order at a window, a lady sat behind a desk and wrote the order down by hand. The next day their van came to the house delivering the goods ordered. It was always a treat to go to that shop because they had a restaurant and we used to have morning coffee, lunch or afternoon tea served by a waitress in a smart uniform with starched cap and apron.

The mode of home deliveries has certainly moved on since the days of the whistling lad on the bicycle and the little van which chugged around country lanes driven by a cheerful man in a brown overall with a leather money bag hanging over his shoulder. Each customer was known personally, and if they hadn't got the cash ready to pay the bill they could be trusted to come to the shop and settle it.

CHAPTER
EIGHT

Children at Play

My friends and I were happy children and in those days when money and resources were limited, we used what was around us to occupy our free time. We had to be imaginative and resourceful so our pastimes varied with the seasons. In the summer we spent most of our time outside in our village, where we had fields, lanes, areas of woodland, a lake, streams, ponds and the River Severn at our disposal. This was our natural playground, where we were free to roam.

I used to call for my friends Anne and Janet Sapsford who lived in Vine Cottage close to Ombersley Court; their father was Bailiff to Lord Sandys so the house, garden and outbuildings came with the job. It was a lovely place for children, and when I was aged seven or eight we could walk across the parkland surrounding the Court, use the footpaths through his Lordship's woodland and play in the gardens when he was not at home. We loved walking down to the lake at Turnmill, from which other paths lead us down to the river. The lake had a dense area of bull-rushes at one end where moorhens nested. Sometimes there were swans or mallards on the lake, and we loved to watch the dragonflies displaying brilliant colours on their fragile wings as they hovered above the water. Once we were very excited to see a large grass snake slithering down the bank into the lake. We were amazed at its speed in the water as it crossed the width of the lake. We had been taught to recognise the scent of the fox; often on these walks we came across it and tried to guess the route it had taken whilst on its nocturnal hunting routes. At night we recognised the sharp brittle bark of a dog fox and the alarming scream of a vixen on heat.

We all had plenty of hobbies. We collected wild flowers and leaves to take home and press; we didn't have proper flower presses, but placed our specimens on old newspaper in layers which were then put underneath a rug or mat on the floor and left to be pressed and dried. When this pressing process was done we stuck them in cheap scrapbooks. I remember my mother helped us to use a botanical reference book so that we could spell the names of the flowers correctly and write them beneath or alongside our specimens. Our efforts were not particularly neat or tidy, but we did learn the names of lots of wild flowers. Anne's parents were pleased to see our efforts and used to give us "prizes"; even Janet (a few years younger) was awarded a prize for something. We had butterfly nets, and pinned the specimens we caught onto thick card. Then we used to try to draw and colour them with crayons. Janet's efforts gave us lots of laughs! We didn't have any means of storing these delicate insects, but we looked up the names in Anne's book and became excited if we found an unusual one.

During school holidays when the weather was warm, we were allowed to take sandwiches or something for lunch and go off together for the whole day. Sometimes we took jam jars with string tied around the neck making a simple handle, which we used to carry home interesting specimens caught in ponds and streams. We played for hours with our shoes and socks off, paddling about in a stream, scooping up water with our jars to see what we had caught. Anne's father had set up an old glass battery accumulator container in which we could tip our pond and stream dipping "finds". We brought home some pondweed and placed this in the bottom with stones and made a sort of aquarium. We liked to watch hatching frogspawn and other pond life. Fallen tree trunks made "bridges" which we would climb onto and walk along when crossing streams in many places around the village. In the park there were some large old beech and chestnut trees with low branches we could jump onto and bounce up and down. A very old oak tree was quite hollow and we could get inside it and climb up onto a hollowed-out branch, where we could sit and hide. We made dens in the woods, and Anne and Janet used to bring comics to read. We talked about the stories and laughed at the antics of cartoon characters in the "Beano" and "Dandy", which I enjoyed particularly because I was not allowed to have comics as my mother disapproved of them.

We collected birds' feathers, and looked into newly built nests, but we did not touch the eggs because we knew the birds would abandon the nest if we did. Boys collected birds' eggs, and competed amongst themselves with their egg collections, swapping and bartering for the less common ones. They were very good at climbing trees.

LEARNING ABOUT WILDLIFE

We were walking across the parkland close to Ombersley Court once, when we found a tiny rabbit in the grass. It was absolutely still, so we touched it and found it was definitely alive. We decided that it had had a terrifying experience; maybe a prowling fox had come across the rabbit family when they were grazing in the lush meadow grass. I picked it up and we took it to the rabbit warrens in bushes at the edge of the wood. When I put it down, it hopped away quickly as if it had recovered from its earlier shock. I wrote to Uncle Mac at BBC "Children's Hour" about this experience and he called to see me one day; I was out with my friends at the time and was *very* disappointed when I heard that I had missed him.

We used to collect caterpillars, and feed them until they had turned into chrysalises. Every year there were bright green ones which ate the leaves of the lime trees in the school playground. These were probably the chrysalis of the Citrus Swallowtail butterfly, which live on Lime (Tiliaceae) or Linden trees with heart shaped leaves and cream flowers.

One of my most memorable experiences was when Anne's father took us to a coppice near to Gardener's Grove Wood, Hadley, where the badgers lived. This coppice had grown in and around a circular dried up pond. The badger setts could be seen around the sloping sides of this, amidst bracken and undergrowth between the trees. We set off at dusk, and when we got near to be coppice we were told to be very quiet; then we settled ourselves in a good position to watch the entrances to several badger setts. Anne's father knew we would have to wait until it was quite dark. Clouds passed over and the moonlight shone into the coppice. We didn't have to wait long before the first badger came up to the entrance to its sett, dug out in the red clay bank. It emerged nose first, sniffing and grunting, followed by another adult badger and two cubs, which were about four months old. Once they were out, an adult badger went back into the sett, and proceeded to shuffle around making lots of grunting noises, coming out backwards, kicking behind it all the dry bedding. They are very clean animals, and regularly have a thorough clear out, sorting it over, gathering fresh bracken and pushing it back down into the sett. The cubs were playing around, and scratching in the soil for grubs and insects, never far away from the parents. Other badger families came out and we watched them all with great interest, taking care not to move or make a sound to disturb them. They gradually went up the banks of the coppice and into the nearby fields to search for roots, grubs and anything edible, which came their way. We were told they will even eat very young rabbits if they find them, and are particularly fond of birds' eggs, especially those of ground nesting birds such as partridge. (I once came across a partridge nest with fourteen eggs in it — they can lay up to twenty — so I kept an eye on it, but found that eggs were being stolen; the hen abandoned that nest). Anne's father had brought a torch, but the moon was bright that night, and we walked home talking about the badgers, with plenty to tell our mothers before we went to bed.

A little danger was more fun. I was in the church wood once when a few lads were climbing up the trees in search of birds' nests, where there was always a rookery. My friends and I thought it would be fun to climb some trees ourselves, as we were fairly good at that; I found a young tree and was soon quite high up, but a lad in a nearby tree kept shouting to me to go up higher. Then a friend climbed up his tree and they caught hold of the ends of branches from my tree and began to pull. The tree bent as they pulled and then released it, and I laughed and laughed; this was great fun! Then they pulled my tree right over as far as they could and let it spring back, catapulting me out squealing loudly! Fortunately I landed in a heap of leaves which had been swept up to clear the pathway to the church, but there was something sharp beneath the leaves and I cut my elbow; otherwise I was unscathed.

Our outdoor play was not without risk, but we did have fun in our own way. We heard stories of boys visiting relatives in the town and being introduced to "tyre rolling". This involved curling up into a large lorry tyre, and then friends stood it up and rolled it along until they let it go down a slope. This was both hilarious and dangerous if the boy in the tyre met a vehicle coming in the opposite direction.

One day I was at Holt Fleet with friends. We had walked up to the locks and were standing around on the riverbank. Some lads came along and began talking to Pim, the lock keeper's son, daring him to walk across the top of the weir. He ran back to the bridge and crossed to the pathway along the opposite bank until we stood where we could view the weir. Pim crossed to the weir on his side from the lock. The River Severn is a deep fast-moving river and pretty wide at that point, but Pim was up for it and took off his shoes and socks and walked across the top of the weir. We thought it was marvellous that he could do that, but he was a strong swimmer and had obviously done it before.

My friend Janet Wood lived at Hilltop House (which was once the Workhouse). Mr. Wood had made a wonderful hanging rope slide for his children; this consisted of a very strong cable attached between a big tree at one end and sloping towards a sturdy tree-trunk at the other end. On to this he had hung a loop of rope threaded through a section of tough rubber tube in the centre, and at the top of the hanging rope was a metal ring, which slid up and down the wire with ease. We had some steps up to a platform where we stood to lean over or sit on the rubber tube section, grasping the rope in each hand, then we jumped off and slid rapidly down the wire to the other end where straw bales broke the impact of our landing. We played for hours on this taking it in turns, and shrieking with delight.

Boys in the village had wooden trolleys made from old wooden soap boxes and scrounged wood off-cuts. These were finished off with old pushchair wheels and a piece of thick string attached to the steering end. The boys got lots of fun from these roughly constructed trolleys, especially when they could be used on a sloping field, track or lane.

Some children liked playing on homemade wooden stilts, and most village children had a swing hung from the branch of an apple tree in the garden; I know I played on mine for hours. I also used to climb into that tree and hang upside down from a higher branch.

Older boys took their younger brothers and friends to fish in the River Severn and the Salwarpe. They used bread, maggots and worms as bait, and caught roach, perch, chub and dace, most of which were thrown back.

In autumn, the hazelnuts ripened, and we all enjoyed eating them straight from the trees; but our families liked to have some to store for winter, so we spent plenty of time collecting nuts. When the sweet chestnuts began to fall, these were also mostly eaten on the spot as they were delicious, and sometimes we took a few for roasting in the embers of the fire. There were walnut trees around and people were always pleased to have them both in their green stage for pickling, and when ripened, to put away for Christmas. I used to collect acorns to take for a neighbour's pig; I loved feeding it with these and hearing the satisfied grunts and crunching as the pig made short work of my offerings.

The conker season came round, and there was no shortage of conkers in our village; the row of big horse-chestnut trees in the centre of the village always yielded a prolific harvest of conkers. We collected them with glee, the aim was to see whose conker lasted the longest and broke the most opponents' conkers. Methods for hardening conkers were discussed by the serious contestants; some put them in the bottom of the cool oven for a while, some pickled them in vinegar. A hole was made through the centre of each conker and a piece of string about a foot long passed through the hole. The conker season began, and we challenged one another to conker fights. The one who had first strike had to say this rhyme first,

"Obley, obley onker, my first conker!
Obley, obley O, my first go!"

Then "champion" conkers emerged — ones which had survived many conker fights and were sometimes sold or exchanged for prized possessions.

When the conker season finished, Mrs. Sanders lost no time in putting marbles in her shop window. She always had a good selection and pocket money was handed over.

Some children devised quite complicated marble games, and played with them a lot until the next "craze" took over.

A large proportion of the adult population were smokers; the tobacco companies knew that cigarette cards boosted sales. We collected them throughout the year, but we tended to spend more time on this hobby when the days were short and indoor occupations took over. Some children had special albums for their cards, others merely stuck their cards into cheap scrap books, or kept them in old shoe boxes. These cards were produced in many categories — aeroplanes, motorcars, trains, ships, film stars, musicians, singers, birds, insects, fish, flowers etc. Cards were swapped, and they were used for games invented by children with big collections.

Boys had crystal set radios with "cat's whisker" receivers. I remember listening to one but the reception was crackly and indistinct. I didn't think much of it.

Some boys had constructed Morse code "tappers" connected to a battery, to tap out the *dot dash* alphabet letters and send each other messages over short distances.

Mr. Sapsford (Anne and Janet's Dad) sometimes had work to do in and around the coach houses and old stables at Ombersley Court, and when all the doors were opened, we loved to go into the coach house and sit in the valuable coaches. Some of these were being stored for the Victoria & Albert Museum, South Kensington, for safety during the war. Queen Victoria's chaise was there. We liked the brougham, a closed coach with velvet, upholstered seating. It was quite dark in there and we made up stories about where we could be going while the horses pulled it along. There was a Landau there too, an open-topped carriage which we imagined would carry beautiful ladies in lovely clothes wearing large hats with ostrich feathers in them. The handsome old Armstrong Siddeley motor car belonging to Lord Sandys, painted yellow with the Sandys crest on the doors, was where we sat imagining we were children of the aristocratic family being driven through the village and waving politely to all the people we knew. That gave us lots of laughs!

In the stables and tack rooms there were other stored "treasures" from the London museum, a bone-shaker bicycle and a penny-farthing bicycle just asking to be tried out! Anne had longer legs than I so she attempted the penny-farthing. We wheeled it out onto the drive and leant it against the wall, then Anne went round into the wood and got up onto the wide top of the wall. I was holding onto the great bicycle and she climbed onto the saddle, placed her feet on the pedals and wobbled away for a short distance before calling *"Help!"* as she steered it back towards the wall. This activity had been accompanied by hoots of laughter and cries of *"Watch out!"* How we escaped injury to ourselves or damage to the penny-farthing was a miracle really. However, we managed it, and she hauled herself off and back onto the top of the wall; then we wheeled it back and left it where we found it. We both had a go on the bone-shaker, with similar determination and bravado, helping each other to alight and dismount; the going was hard and much effort went into the pedalling — all good fun on a cold winter's day! What would the curators of the great museum have said if they had seen us in action? Fortunately no harm was done.

THE WORKHOUSE IN OMBERSLEY VILLAGE

Building a Workhouse was a provision of the Church Act of 1814. Trustees of the Church Act had agreed to provide a workhouse in Ombersley, and it was built in

Hog Lane, now known as Hill Top Lane and the building remains there as a private house known as "Hill Top House". A man named Mr. Pulley was the Assistant Overseer of the Poor and he collected the rates and administered the Poor Laws. In 1827 he was given the job of Governor of the Workhouse at a salary of £36 per annum plus living accommodation, a garden, ten tons of coal and food. He was also allowed 3/6d (three shillings and six pennies) for journeys under ten miles and 7½d (seven pence and one half-penny) for each extra mile. To feed and keep the inmates, he received 3/- (three shillings) per person per week.

It was intended that the Workhouse was run to be self-sufficient and profitable, so as to relieve the burden on the ratepayers. Inmates were expected to earn their keep. Unfortunately this didn't happen, the inmates there were elderly, seriously ill or disabled people as well as unmarried mothers and their children. One of the earliest resolutions for running the Workhouse was *Not to separate bastard children from their mothers before seven years*. They had 15 to 20 permanent residents, and others were taken in for short periods when they were out of work, or destitute for other reasons. Usually about 24 inmates resided there.

Ombersley Workhouse was not set up as a bleak, unwelcoming place like many other such places. It was furnished in a basic way with beds, bed mats, blankets and sheets, pewter and tin plates and utensils, even a clothes line which cost five shillings (out of the Rates). Occasionally shoes and clothes were purchased as well as medicines. Funeral expenses were paid. They

69

received three meals a day, of strictly measured portions for able bodied inmates:

Men had 21ozs. bread per day
+ 1½pints gruel per day and 1½oz. cheese for supper.

Women had 17ozs. bread per day
+ 1½pints gruel per day and 1½oz. cheese for supper.

The midday meal on Sunday, Monday, Wednesday, Friday — 7ozs bread + 2ozs. cheese for men.

The midday meal on Sunday, Monday, Wednesday, Friday — 6ozs bread + 1½ozs. cheese for women.

The midday meal on Tuesday — ¾lb. vegetables + 8ozs. meat for men and women.

The midday meal on Thursday — 1½pints. Soup + 6ozs. bread men and 5ozs. bread women.

The midday meal on Saturday — ¾lb. vegetables + 5ozs. cooked bacon men — 4ozs. women.

Children over 9 years were given the same quantities as women.

Old people were allowed 1oz. tea, 5oz. butter and 7oz. sugar in lieu of gruel.

Gruel — to make 1½ pints mix 3 dessertspoons of groats or fine oatmeal with a little cold water, add 1½ pints boiling water and boil for 10 minutes, sugar or salt may be added.

In the village there were a hundred or so people on permanent benefit, and as many who received occasional relief. The Workhouse may not have been a cheaper way of helping the poor. They tried to reduce costs to the ratepayers; in one case a son was offered a shilling a week to take his father home. A family from a nearby village were taken in for four shillings a week, paid from the parish rates, but that venture lasted only five weeks and was not repeated. Mr. Pulley was dismissed in 1832, but he was slow to go and had to be compensated for the fruit trees he had planted. In 1833 the cost of feeding and keeping each inmate was reduced to 10d. per week. It must have been a blessing to the parish officers when the Poor Law Amendment Act of 1834 was passed. The Ombersley Workhouse closed on 12th November 1836.

CHAPTER
NINE

Children at Work

When pea-picking time came around, some children were taken out of school to go to the pea fields with their mothers. This usually took place during the school summer holidays, but if the crops were ready earlier the lorries to transport pickers to various farms called at the school where older children and their mothers were waiting before the school day began. Out in the fields the peas were weighed and pickers were paid a small amount for each "pot" picked at the end of the day.

When the blackberries were ripe in the hedgerows near to our school, our teachers sometimes took us out to pick them. We shared baskets and picked as many as we could reach. The blackberries were sent to the dinner ladies who cooked our school dinners in the Memorial Hall kitchen. Children were encouraged to pick up windfall apples and to collect any surplus fruit from neighbours and bring it to school. The school dinner cooks made good use of it all and made jam for use in winter.

The older children were also allowed out of school for spud lifting. This was heavy work; they lifted the potatoes by hand and fork and earned a little money.

For seven years the senior pupils of Ombersley school made this contribution to the war effort.

Families who had relatives living in the towns told us that schoolboys were volunteering to work in the coalmines as "Bevin Boys". Ernest Bevin had won the right to employ a proportion of the young men called up for National Service to work in the mines instead of joining the armed forces. They didn't all have to work at the coalface. Indeed wartime experiences brought friendships between people from very different social backgrounds.

When mothers and relatives went in the lorry to the hop yards at hoppicking time, the children went with them. The smell of the ripe hops when they are being picked is just wonderful. I didn't go hop picking, but for some families it was an annual social event. Some of them brought tents and camped out near the hop-yards. They used to come in the shop and say they never slept as well at home; the open air work and the smell of the hops made them all sleep soundly. Some women made "hop pillows" to take home, which were thought to be good for people who didn't sleep well. They loved the camaraderie, meeting folk from Worcester and Birmingham who came every year to have a holiday and earn some money. Some used to say that it paid for new shoes.

I know someone who, as a schoolboy, used to go with his mother when she cleaned offices in the centre of Worcester. It was his job to empty all the waste paper baskets, collect up the sacks of paper and trundle them down to the rag and paper merchants by the river. He

73

sold this paper waste for about 1/- (one shilling) for his cartful.

When he was eleven he got a job working for Elt's Shoe Shop in the Shambles in Worcester. He used to work every day after school and on Saturdays, and was paid 6/- per week. He got on really well there and when he told the boss he would like to buy a particular pair of shoes for himself but didn't have enough money, the boss said he could have the shoes and they would deduct sixpence a week from his pay. This job eventually led him to a full time position at the shop when he left school.

I used to earn a little pocket money at our shop by doing a variety of jobs, weighing up bags of washing soda, and taking all the empty biscuit tins out to the lorry when a new delivery arrived. I had learned to chop firewood, and Grandma gave me sixpence when I filled a basket for her. I was sometimes asked to fill customers' paraffin cans and I used to bring in bars of various types of soap from the outside store and fill the shelves beneath the counter in the shop.

Some of the older boys who worked on farms after school, at weekends and in the holidays, earned a little money. Their pay was often supplemented by being allowed to catch as many rabbits as they could on their employers' land. Some lads kept ferrets and had dogs trained as rabbit catchers. They used to talk about this sport at school. They all enjoyed it and were competitive. They learned so much about the countryside and probably about the art of poaching too! They would get two shillings or even two and sixpence each for good rabbits. The women-folk made rabbit stew and rabbit pies, and many thought these meals were delicious. Grandma used to say that a good rabbit stew should have plenty of bacon hock in it as well as onions, seasoning and other root vegetables. Such wholesome, nutritious meals were frequently served up in villages like ours.

My father was always proud of his vegetable garden, in which he grew outdoor tomatoes. Each plant had a flower pot set into the ground by the base of the main stem, so that he could fill the pot with water and sometimes with a mixture of his "special fertiliser", taking it to the roots of each plant. The fertiliser was made from sheep droppings, and I used to go with him to help pick up the dried sheep droppings and put them in a sack. It wasn't very pleasant when we picked up a soft one! The droppings were then emptied into a wooden barrel and covered with water, and Daddy used to put a lid on the barrel, because it attracted flies in the warm weather. This natural fertiliser gave off quite a strong smell, but it worked very well indeed as we had very good tomatoes and other vegetables.

CHAPTER
TEN

A Main Road View
of Village Life

The old saying "If you sit in the same position at the roadside for long enough the rest of the world will pass before you" must be true. There was usually some activity on the road through Ombersley; ours was very much a living village even when times were hard. People passed up and down the main road as they went about their daily lives throughout the seasons. Some motorised traffic passed through; the doctor, vicar, shopkeepers, farmers and better-off people in the village owned cars, vans and lorries. Most people relied upon the bus service for transport when they made long journeys; otherwise they walked, cycled and used horse-drawn vehicles, especially when petrol was rationed.

I was always interested when one of the farmers came along with a horse and cart, and occasionally there were deliveries to the public houses by brewers' drays. The handsome dray horses whose harnesses hung with brightly polished horse brasses were certainly a memorable sight. I remember when one such dray was waiting outside *The King's Arms*. I was with my father, admiring the horse when Charlie Morris came out to speak to the driver. Always the joker, Charlie asked. "What is the difference between a war horse and a dray horse?" The drayman couldn't answer the question so Charlie said "The war horse darts into the fray! The dray horse . . ." leaving us to finish the sentence. I needed some help — my vocabulary of "naughty words" was very limited.

The knife grinder sometimes trundled into the village, ringing his bell to let people know he was there. His brightly painted and gilded grinding machine was set on wheels and he trundled this along from one place to another, earning his living by sharpening blades of all shapes and sizes. I once rushed into the house and grabbed a table knife from Grandmother's cutlery drawer. I took it out and stood watching while he duly sharpened the blade, then he went into the shop to ask for payment. I was in double trouble then, receiving a smack from Aunty Win who had paid him from the till and another smack from Grandma because the stainless steel blades of that bone-handled cutlery set were never sharpened.

A group of young lads were usually hanging around beneath the horse-chestnut tree by the island; jolly lads, some had bicycles propped against the Church Field fence, others had walked to this favourite meeting place. They talked and sometimes called out rude remarks to passers by, this was their pitch for having a laugh.

Women walked along carrying baskets or bags when they had visited the village shops. Sometimes they carried produce from their gardens to exchange with friends and neighbours, sharing what they had and making do with the little they could buy when food was rationed. Women pushed prams and rode on bicycles. Some had jobs in the big houses around the village, where they cleaned and cooked for the "snobs" as they referred to the gentry, wealthy people and those whose circumstances and life experience was different to their own. There were several large houses near the village where ex-forces officers lived with their families (always retaining their rank — being known as Colonel, Major, Commander, Brigadier etc.) People didn't hesitate to discuss the business of others. There was plenty of evidence of jealousy, and sometimes quite cruel comments were bandied around.

The vicar often walked around the village, and one day he was visiting people in Rax Lane and called at a cottage for some parochial reason. Receiving no response at the front door, he walked around to the back. The door was open, he stepped inside. Just as he was about to call out the name of the occupant, he looked around to where the large woman of the house stood stripped to the waist, having a wash at the kitchen sink. She was startled, and he opened his mouth to speak just as she picked up the bowl of soapy water and threw it over him! No doubt she yelled a few choice obscenities at him as she did so; her voice was loud, and she was a field worker known for fighting. A dripping wet vicar walked back down the lane and home through the village, much to the amusement of those who saw him! That story went around the village with great speed, the way such stories always did.

Near to the *Cross Keys* public house there was a tiny shop and cottage called "The Gallies" where you could have shoes repaired and buy newspapers. The smell of newly baked bread wafting from France's Bakery was always good; they also sold buns and cakes. Brookes' shop further along the road, opposite the field surrounding the village hall, sold fresh fruit and vegetables, but we couldn't get bananas or oranges during the war.

The Sansome family of Claines delivered milk to the village by horse and cart; people still remember how the horse refused to budge when they reached the *Cross Keys* public house until he had been given a drink of beer. No doubt this sustained him for his return journey to Claines — about 3½ miles.

There were more people walking about on Sundays when they went to church, and at times people waited at the bus stops to catch the 315 bus into Worcester, or to other villages between the village and Kidderminster. My father used that bus sometimes to go to work in Hartlebury. When Mum took me to Birmingham each month to see a Paediatric Dental Specialist, our journey began on the 315 Kidderminster bus.

I particularly remember one winter Sunday when I was about eight years old, and my friends and I had been to Sunday School. Grandma had bought me a navy blue pilot cloth winter coat and a cerise coloured felt hat and I was wearing them for the first time on that day. We decided to go and pick snowdrops growing by the stream running along in the strip of woodland bordering the parkland around Ombersley Court. We knew just the spot where lots of lovely snowdrops grew and a natural "bridge" in the form of a fallen tree, spanned the stream. I was last to walk over this with a little bunch of snowdrops in my hand. I slipped and fell into the muddy water, the dark mud clung to my woollen coat and I was in an awful state. My friends laughed and hauled me up the bank out of the stinking water, I quickly discovered that the soak-away drains from nearby cottages emptied into that stream.

My feet, legs and most of my lovely new coat were coated with thick sticky, very smelly mud and I had to walk back through the village to get home. I prayed that the congregation were still in church, and that the local lads had not taken up their position under the chestnut-tree. Unfortunately for me, the lads were there and the sight of me in that awful state caused them much amusement, they shouted out "Where've you bin Rosie?" "Coo, Rosie's mucky!" "Sh★★★y Rosie!" Hoots of laughter, then "Wait till you get home!" I began to cry, my feet and legs were black and muddy, I was in such a sorry state! They laughed more loudly as I squelched by, tears streaming down my face and my hat askew.

There was a small chapel in the lane running behind the Memorial Hall, and sometimes on Sundays a lady came there from Worcester to play the piano and lead the hymn singing for the service. She always had some time with the children after the service when the adults went out to talk. We sang, "I'm *H-A-P-P-Y*, I am, I am,

I know I am, I'm *H-A-P-P-Y*" and "Jesus wants me for a sunbeam." She had a repertoire of tunes for children, and we particularly liked the "One finger, one thumb, keep moving" one which we joined in with the movements until we were exhausted when it came to the end, "One finger, one thumb, one arm, one leg, stand up, sit down keep moving, and we will all be merry and bright!" She arrived by car with a minister and usually wore a dress, coat and hat in a vivid lilac colour, and had a happy smiling face and a hearty way of leading the singing.

One day I was walking up the road on my way to fetch bread from the bakery. Coming towards me was "Charlie the bear", I was scared and crossed the road to walk on the other side. Charlie seemed quite a big man, he wore an ex-army great-coat and probably a jacket underneath it. His hat was pulled down on his head and his bushy brown beard and hair covered his face and neck. The children used to make up stories about Charlie, saying he had hair all over his body, even on his feet. They said his ancestors were part bear and part man. Others made out he was really "Superman" in disguise (Superman first appeared in children's' comics in 1938). Charlie lived in a pigsty at the back of the *Fruiterer's Arms* in Uphampton Lane with the permission of Mr. May the landlord, Charlie did some work for him and managed to get other casual work in the area.

It was always quite exciting when a charabanc or two arrived at the village school to take the children on an outing to Weston-Super-Mare or Barry Island. Parents came to wave them off, and these outings were always the topic of conversation before and after the event. Every detail was recounted about what children had seen in the "What the butler saw" type of peep-show machines on the pier, or things they had won in the fun-fair. There were always a few funny mishaps such as the time when one of the teachers sat on a child's ice cream cornet, or the odd unfortunate incident. Once a child was lost and eventually found locked in a public lavatory, though generally nothing serious occurred and all (except those who were travel sick), had a good time.

Convoys of American troops passed through the village occasionally, which was always exciting for the children who were around. They ran to the roadside and called out to the troops sitting in the back of the lorries "Got any gum, chum?" The Yanks laughed and threw out packets of biscuits and gum. On one such occasion — I was on the pavement outside our shop with a couple of friends all waving to the American convoy and calling out. I unbuckled my kilt, and waved it above my head, standing there laughing and calling to the Yanks in my jumper and knickers! They responded with a shower of assorted packets and I received a leg smacking when Mother spotted my antics!

Lorries came to the weighbridge by the island to have their loads of hay, straw, sugar beet, cabbages, potatoes and other root crops weighed. Mr. Rea came across from his garage and carpentry sheds, unlocked the weighing station and filled out the forms for the drivers.

The church verger, Wilf Dyson, frequently cycled from his house to the school, as he also had the job of school caretaker. In the winter he had to get up to the school and light the fires in all the classrooms before the school day began; then he cleaned out the ashes at the end of each day and laid the fires for the next morning, filling buckets of coal so that the fires could be kept going throughout the day. He was a busy man and had plenty to do around the church and school.

I was about seven years old when I was sent on an errand to a small house and, being unable to make anyone hear at the front door, I went around to the back. The day was warm and sunny and the open door indicated that someone was at home. I called and tapped on the door, noises came from within, but nobody appeared. I looked down the garden and couldn't see anyone there, so I stepped inside, into a room combining both kitchen and living room. There, on an old maroon velvet chaise longue, beneath the window, lay a child with an abnormal head and face. It was making strange noises, obviously severely mentally and physically handicapped. I gasped with shock, ran out crying and kept running. I arrived home obviously upset; I clung to my mother and tried to tell her what I had seen. She was probably surprised, but didn't say much about it at the time.

Several years later I was told that the couple who lived there were not a married couple as we had always thought, but brother and sister. They left the village suddenly because the woman was pregnant again. Incest has always been there below the societal surface.

Poverty, large families and poor housing meant that some families lived in overcrowded homes. In villages it was not unusual to find small, two-up and two-down cottages inhabited by families of six to ten children, living in disorderly squalor. Children slept in the same room and often in the same bed as their parents; their way of life didn't allow for modesty. Social historians have recorded that mixed sex siblings of all ages shared beds. In such circumstances chastity and normal decency didn't exist, they thought there was nothing wrong with incest, and they laughed and teased one another about it. Father and daughter, brother and sister relations were known about; public efforts to provide better housing was the primary response.

CHAPTER
ELEVEN
School Days

The school had three entrance porches (with pegs for coats) leading to classrooms. All classrooms were interlinking, the windows were large and each room had a big fireplace for the coal fires used for winter heating. Senior pupils were in the classroom used by Mr. Thomas E. Styles, the Headmaster (school-leaving age in 1942 was 14 years). That room had a porch entrance on the south side of the school and inter-communicating doors to classrooms on both sides. Mr. Cyril Booking's classroom was on the east side and that room was partitioned off from Mr. Styles's room by a wall of folding screen sections. Mr. Brooking was in the RAF from 1939-45. When the screens were pushed back the combined classroom space could be used for whole school assemblies.

Mrs. Edith Styles used the classroom at the front of the building and Miss Smith had the infants' classroom, the porch to which is adjacent to the Headmaster's house on the Droitwich side of the building.

The pupils' lavatories and shelters with space for bicycles stood at the back of the playground areas. The garage for the Headmaster's car stood at the back of the playground; a pathway between it and the shelters led to the Headmaster's garden.

Attendance at the village school was never so good in the winter months, as children went down with coughs, colds and sore throats, and the germs spread throughout the school. Many children came to school with heavy colds; it was warmer in the classrooms than at home. Pupils arrived at school in wet clothing, and sometimes stood in front of the fire to dry out, some didn't have Wellington boots, their wet boots and shoes were removed and put near the fire, socks draped over the fire-guard. Newspaper was provided for those whose socks and shoes were drying, they placed it beneath the desks to put their feet on. In the Infants' classroom, if a child had an accident and wet their pants or knickers, they had to stand in front of the fire until their clothing had dried out. The smell of steamy drying urine was not pleasant!

OUR HEADMASTER

On Sundays my friends and I went up to the organ gallery in St. Andrew's church, where our Sunday School teacher gave us a short lesson. We sat in a row of seats at the front of the gallery with the organ behind us. Mr. Styles, known by everyone as Tommy Styles and by the children as "The Boss", was also church organist and choirmaster. Sunday School always ended just before he arrived to open up the organ in readiness for the service, and a boy was paid to pump the organ bellows. We were allowed to leave the church before the Vicar's sermon, and once outside, we walked through the church wood, sometimes pausing to sit on a fallen tree and talk. Talk of events at school were frequent topics; I arrived home once and told my mother the one about when Tommy Styles was *so angry* with a boy misbehaving that he took his glass eye out and aimed it at the lad. I don't think she believed it, but it made her laugh!

Another story was about naughty Derek Hayes, who Mr. Styles caned. Derek ran out of school and across the fields to his home in Hay Lane, crying all the way. Granny Hayes heard his tearful account and lost no time in marching up to the school, broom in hand, to confront "the Boss". The story went that she shouted at him "Don't you *ever* lay a finger on our Derek again, I warns yer!" She was awesome when roused, and my Sunday School friends insisted that she chased him into the playground threatening him with her broom. The picture conjured up of this small sinewy woman, who always wore a black apron, and tied her grey hair in a tight knot at the back of her head, chasing the Boss with her broom made us all laugh. No doubt it was exaggerated, probably embellished a little further each time it was gleefully passed on.

Thomas Ernest Styles was a bald-headed robust man whose powerful personality and deep resonant voice made him unmistakable. He had lost the sight of one eye, but his remaining bloodshot and bulging brown eye didn't miss a thing! He was *The Boss*, in every sense of the word; his powerful presence within the

87

school was obvious to everyone. An essay written by an ex pupil describes him thus . . .

". . . he dominated his small school, his subordinate teaching staff, his wary captive pupils. With the morning light polishing his bald head and its half circle of grey frizz, he would make his way through the classrooms, the sound and vibration of his footsteps on the rough floorboards, warning of his approach . . ."

(an unpublished essay *Pen Portrait of a Person Well Remembered* by the late Diana Jasinski.)

Discipline was strict and sometimes painful; the Boss had a good supply of canes delivered at the beginning of each school year. Many of those were probably worn out more by his habit of rapping them on the desk for attention than by administering punishments.

MY FIRST DAY AT SCHOOL

My fifth birthday was on 10th July 1942, so I was due to begin school in September of that year. My first day arrived, I couldn't eat much of my small breakfast, I was very nervous. My older Sunday School friends had told me about their school experiences; they knew they had got me worried, and enjoyed telling me about the The Boss's methods of maintaining discipline.

I gathered that he was strict and made regular use of the cane. One day Beryl, a girl in Mr. Styles's class, was upset because he was very angry with a boy named Roy and was threatening to cane him. Beryl told me that the Boss was red in the face, standing over Roy and shouting loudly. She left her seat and went to the front of the room where she grabbed both his canes and threw them onto the fire. They burned immediately and so she was in trouble too! She had to stay after school and stand for half an hour with her hands on her head. No doubt Roy didn't escape the caning; the Boss would have found another cane!

I heard that other teachers had canes too, but tended to smack hands and legs by hand or with a ruler, if one was nearby. My apprehension had steadily increased; I walked at my mother's side up to the school. At the gate I grabbed her hand and we went round to the infants' classroom. Other mothers with children were waiting to go in. Mr. Styles stood in the doorway of that entrance and greeted all the new pupils. The mothers walked away and the children went through the porch to meet Miss Smith and then to go into her classroom.

So there I was, holding my mother's hand, waiting to go into school on that first day. Mrs. Dyson stood in front of us holding Terry's hand; he was beginning to cry. When they reached Mr. Styles, Terry was audibly unhappy and clinging to his mother, who was trying to reassure him. Mr. Styles spoke to Mrs. Dyson, smiled, and lifted Terry up holding him tightly beneath his armpits. Terry, now bawling loudly, was jerked up as high as the Headmaster's arms could reach and then rapidly bounced down to the floor. This took Terry's breath away momentarily, but as soon as Mr. Styles let go of him he continued crying. The upward jerk and bounce down movements continued, Terry emitting louder bawls between them. I was scared, I hung on to mother's hand as we stood watching. Eventually Mrs. Dyson took Terry away; his cries could be heard as they walked up the playground. I like to think that Miss Smith arranged a more gentle reception for Terry on another day, for he did join our class a day or two later.

LESSONS AND TEACHING METHODS

I had already learned to read nursery rhymes and short stories before I went to school. Miss Smith's careful rote method of teaching the alphabet and basic reading became somewhat tedious for me; I wanted to get on with more interesting things. I enjoyed writing and could write my name and address and simple short sentences, and always wanted to add a little drawing to my work. I was not so good at arithmetic and needed lots of practice with tables; we chanted our tables over and over again. The rote system, i.e. use of the blackboard and organised chanting, played a huge part in the teaching methods used in schools at that time. Our teachers stood at their blackboards, cane in hand, pointing and saying what was written, then telling the class to repeat aloud as the pointing continued, endless pedantic repetition now long outmoded.

Our written work was done first on slates with chalk then progressing to exercise books with cheap ruled rough paper and pencils. We began with pothooks and *a b c*; sometimes Miss Smith would lean over and guide our hands. She always smelled of lavender. Later on we were taught to write with pens and ink — a messy business! The wooden desks had inkwells, so an "ink monitor" was appointed to keep the white china inkwells filled. Our work was marked, errors pointed out and marks called out by pupils so that the teachers could enter them into record books.

Left-handedness was *not* allowed. All children had to use their right hands for writing, cutting out, drawing and painting etc. From the beginning the weakest, slowest pupils were verbally chastised and sometimes punished. I shall always remember a little girl in my class named Josie Betts being made to stand in the corner with a dunce's hat on her head! She cried. This happened several times; I used to go and sit with her outside when playtime came and try to cheer her up or lend her my skipping rope.

All pupils were taught reading, writing and arithmetic daily and given a smattering of other subjects and activities on the curriculum. All classes were taught by the "chalk and talk" method, with lots of copying from the board. Physical Education took place on the playground or on the Memorial Hall playing field. Sometimes Mrs. Styles would take her class out to sit in the grassy field and read their books. Mr. Styles used to take the senior boys into his garden, where they learned how to dig, weed and hoe. They sometimes went there to continue their practical gardening skills unsupervised. The garden was kept in tiptop order, Mr. Dyson sometimes helped too. I was taken into the garden with two other girls and shown how to pick thyme for Mrs. Styles. We returned to the classroom with the thyme sprigs and helped the others to strip the leaves from those and sprigs of other herbs she wanted to preserve. Art was an opportunity for free expression rather than a taught subject. Lessons were delivered with a constant whole class approach, I can't remember any attempts to stretch the brighter pupils or address the needs of the slow learners or those with difficulties.

School assemblies were a diversion for some hymn singing, and short talks from the Boss who rapped his cane on the desk loudly if anyone was not paying attention. The vicar sometimes came to talk to us. The assembly time seemed longer on those occasions. Once we had a visit from a Christian missionary, a large exotic, coloured lady who wore brightly coloured clothes and strings of beads around her neck. Her hair was tied up in a multi-coloured turban and she had big dangling earrings. She talked to us about where she came from and children in that country. Then she played the piano with great energy, thumping out hymns we didn't know. They were more like songs and she got us all to sing choruses and clap our hands. She was great fun; we were sorry when her visit ended and it was home time. We walked out of school talking about her, and when we approached the village island, there she was waving to us! She asked us to go and sit with her beneath a horse chestnut tree in the field, and when we were settled she told us some stories about her country and we did more singing and clapping. It wasn't quite the same without the piano, but her visit was a memorable experience and she was certainly a good teacher. She had come to the village in a horse-drawn caravan which was parked in Church Lane.

Like the curate's egg, school was good in parts. Mr. and Mrs. Styles had a terrier dog whose name was "Skipper"; his smooth coat was mainly white with patches of brown and black. He barked a lot and had to be kept away from the children. He was a very aggressive and snappy dog and couldn't be trusted; children had been bitten by him in the past!

I usually went home for my midday meal because I disliked the school dinners cooked at the Memorial Hall; several village women worked in the kitchen there cooking and serving school meals. At lunch times the teachers accompanied the children, walking in orderly crocodiles, to the Memorial Hall along the main road, keeping strictly to the pavements. In summer when the ground was dry, they took a shortcut from the school across the fields and down to the main road opposite the entrance to the Memorial Hall playing field.

I absolutely hated using the smelly school lavatories. They were outside behind the main school building and had no running water. The boys and girls sides were separate, but the boys' urinal was outside their covered area of lavatory cubicles. When entering the girls' lavatories we could sometimes see the top of a head or heads as they stood relieving themselves. They shouted rude things to us and the big boys thought it a great joke if they could aim some water (or pee) over at us! On both sides there was a small sink with a cold-water tap in the shelter areas (I do not recall seeing a towel) but no one bothered to wash their hands! We drank from that tap and fetched water from it in jam jars when it was needed for painting or fresh flowers brought in by pupils for the classrooms.

The lavatory cubicles had wooden doors and wooden seats, a roll of hard non-absorbent toilet paper hung from string on the back of each door; often there was none left. The smell was always foul and worse in warm weather. The caretaker, Wilf Dyson, cleaned and emptied the toilet buckets regularly, and swilled the floors down with strong disinfectant. The buckets were emptied in a place provided in the garden behind the shelters. I avoided using the lavatories as much as I could.

At the village school we saved all the cardboard tops from the small bottles we were given at playtime. These were washed and dried and then we covered them with raffia in natural, dark blue, red, and green colours, threading it on blunt ended needles with large eyes using a button-hole stitch going in and out of the central hole until the cardboard disc was covered. These covered discs were then sewn together in patterns making shopping bags, tablemats, and magazine covers. I made a cover for the *Radio Times*, the front and back pages fitted perfectly into the pockets at either end protecting the magazine. I gave it to my Aunty Glad who lived in Harborne, Birmingham.

She was very pleased with it and used it for the next decade or so.

WINTER — DAMP CLOTHES, FROZEN MILK AND FUN

In winter the classroom fires burned away keeping us warm. The big fire guards were used to dry wet coats, hats and gloves; classroom windows steamed up and a smell of (often none too clean) clothing drying out permeated through the school. All the year round we had school milk in ⅓ pint bottles at mid-morning break times. In winter it was placed near to the fire to warm up and even to thaw out if it was frozen on very frosty mornings. Winters seemed to be very cold; in 1947 we had deep snow and for a short time children who walked to school from the Hamptons, Holt Fleet and Hadley couldn't get to school. The road to Droitwich was blocked and prisoners of war from a camp near Droitwich dug a pathway through to the island at Ombersley. I once had to wear my mother's fur-lined boots to school because my shoes were wet. These were much too large for my little feet, but I had several pairs of socks on and hobbled up to school in them! I was so embarrassed, I didn't wear them again.

The school was only closed for a short time due to this bad weather, when it re-opened the snow had been swept back towards the outer edges of the playgrounds, leaving pathways around the school buildings clear. However, we made good use of the remaining snow, snowball fights began, and the boys lost no time in making slides to skid along. Shrieks of joy rang out at these activities, bringing the Boss out to marshal us into the shelters where we were told sternly not to throw snowballs, slide, or get into the snow. We had to wait there until the bell was rung, so we sat on the long benches at the back of the shelters, or just stood around talking. When we were allowed to go into the classrooms there were more wet clothes to be dried around the fires.

The wooden floors of all the classrooms rang with the sound of hardsoled boots and shoes. Chalk dust from the blackboards and slates in the infants' room was always in the air. The old wooden desks had grooves along the top for pens and pencils and an ink-well on the right hand side. The hinged lids had marks made on them by former pupils, initials and drawings deeply drawn into the wood. Our school desks and hard wooden benches and chairs were polished smooth, though this was not a waxed polish patina, rather a mellowing from constant use. There was always a banging of desk lids at the end of lessons when books were put away, and other books brought out. Fingers were pinched under desk lids from time to time, knuckles were rapped for banging lids, pupils were pushed off benches onto the floor, or fell off their chairs; it was inevitable that minor classroom accidents and injuries were experienced, it was all part of the course.

PLAYTIMES

Playtimes in fine weather were good, we played hop-scotch, and skipping, sometimes using a long rope so that two or three people could skip while two others turned the rope. Our skipping was usually accompanied by singing or chanting rhymes, such as *Oranges and Lemons* and *One two buckle my shoe*. Once we were doing that when Teddy May and some of the big boys came round to our side of the playground and took the rope off us, then they ran around us with it and tied it up, laughing all the time. I arrived home with a rope burn on my arm, Grandma put some ointment on it and bound it up. Next day it looked quite nasty, so Mother told me to show it to Mr. Styles and tell him how it had happened. When he came into our classroom, I showed him my arm, and he sent for Teddy May, showed him what he had caused, extracted an apology from him and took him away to share some disciplinary action with the other lads involved!

One particular mid-afternoon playtime on a sunny summer day a game of *The Farmer Wants a Wife* began; the moving circle of children holding hands grew until whole classes were in the circle, and soon it expanded even more when the older children from the other side of the playground also joined in; it went rather like this:

The children link hands, trot round and sing . . .

Here comes the farmer,
Here comes the farmer,
E, I, O, U, here comes the farmer.

They stop moving, choose a "farmer" (sometimes by the "eeny meeny miny mo" process) or the tallest boy in the circle, he stands in the middle of the circle. The singing and trotting continues . . .

The farmer wants a wife,
The farmer wants a wife,
E, I, O, U, the farmer wants a wife.

The farmer chooses his wife and she joins him to stand in the middle, then it is the wife's turn and she wants — *a child* . . .

The wife wants a child — etc. etc.

The game progresses in this way until any number of others are now standing in the middle — *horse, cow, pig, goose, cockerel, hen,* and lastly *dog,*

Ending with . . .

the dog wants a bone,

and so forth, followed by . . .

We all touch the bone,
We all touch the bone,
E, I, O, U, we all touch the bone.

Then the whole circle moves inwards so that everyone can touch *the bone* — this always caused lots of laughter and quite a bit of pushing and shoving!

This turned out to be quite a unique occasion — all the teachers and Mr. Styles joined the circle and the game went on until it was time to go home! We were all so happy.

ERRANDS FOR THE HEADMASTER

Mr. Styles sometimes came to me during lesson times and sent me on an errand to our shop for his pipe tobacco or cigarettes. He would scribble a note on a piece of paper and say "Go down to your shop and ask them to send me this, don't be long!" The cost of his tobacco or cigarettes would be put on the bill, so I was never given any money to pay for these things.

I was on my way back to school one warm summer afternoon; I had taken his note to the shop and carried his requirements in a paper bag. I walked up Hilltop Lane, watching butterflies and bumble bees on the wild flowers in the hedgerows. When I came to the little footpath leading past the back of Mrs. Davis's house, I noticed a lot of pretty white flowers. I decided to pick a bunch of these to take back to school, and arranged them with some foliage into a nice little bunch, breaking off a small twig and skinning off a strip of the outer layer to tie around my "posy".

When I arrived at Mr. Styles's desk in the big classroom he was *not* pleased. I had been away too long and he didn't like the flowers I handed to him with his paper bag. He said "Take them away, they stink, you should know this is wild garlic!" I was not asked to run one of his errands again!

A BRIEF NOTE ABOUT THE HISTORY AND ACCOMMODATION OF THE VILLAGE SCHOOL

Ombersley Elementary School, sometimes referred to as "The Lloyds' School". After the Elementary Education Act 1870 it was obvious that a new school was needed, and many schemes were proposed. Lloyds Educational Foundation became the principal charitable trust finally involved with funding for building the school. A Government grant was made in 1873, and Lord Sandys gave the plot of land. An architect named Rowe was commissioned to draw up plans for the school and Mr. Beard the building contractor completed the contract in 1876, including the headmaster's residence.

CHAPTER TWELVE

Some Light Relief was Essential

The news on the radio sometimes got people down; occasional moans and complaints about the general state of things were largely outweighed by the collective spirit and determination to keep smiling through. Maintaining the traditional "stiff upper lip" was all very well, but some light relief was called for. Not many folk could afford to go out of the village for entertainment, so the villagers organised their own social entertainment. The Memorial Hall vibrated with life and laughter and the worries of wartime could be temporarily forgotten.

DANCE NIGHTS

My father never missed the dance evenings. When it was an evening dress occasion he dressed carefully in his tailor-made black suit (much used in his former life in London). When he had brushed and pressed it he cleaned his patent leather dancing shoes using the cream from the top of the milk. His evening shirt was always sent to the laundry after use to be professionally starched and ironed. I remember him coming downstairs wearing his black trousers with the silk stripe down the sides and his collarless shirt. He had put in his gold cufflinks, and carried his collar studs and bow tie; standing before the mirror above the living room mantelpiece, he attached the collar, put the black tie around his neck and quickly tied a perfect bow with practiced skill. Then he put on his jacket with the satin lapels. He would whistle and sing while he dressed and once he even did a little tap dance on the kitchen floor when he had tied his shoelaces. Daddy was in good spirits on these occasions, but my mother didn't join in. She chose to stay at home with me and listen to the radio or read. I would have been just as happy staying with Grandma at the shop. Daddy used to partner the vicar's housekeeper Miss Daisy Swan. I expect she was also smartly dressed; people took care of their good pre-war clothing.

Not all dance nights were evening dress occasions; informal dances with gramophone music drew people in. Old Time Dancing lessons were organised by Mr. and Mrs. Ewers, professional dancing instructors from Worcester. They brought their own music — a gramophone with extra amplifiers and a selection of dance music records. Everyone learned the full range of Old Time dances including *Old Time Waltz, St Bernard's Waltz, Square Tango, Military Two-step, Valeta, Gay Gordons* and others. The progressive dances were always good fun and everyone enjoyed changing partners. The *Gay Gordons* was usually danced by those who enjoyed the energetic, boisterous fun of this Scottish dance, which usually preceded the interval when refreshments were served, and the dancers could sit down, or walk outside to cool off. These were popular regular social evenings, married couples and single people joined in, it was an opportunity to forget the war and everyday problems. There was usually a *Ladies' Excuse Me* dance, which entitled ladies to separate couples dancing together. It worked very well and everyone had a laugh. Dance evenings always ended with a waltz at the end; married couples always danced together for this and budding relationships between the single people were noted!

THE VILLAGE CONCERT

The village concert party put on an annual event. Aunty Win and Uncle John always sang one of their duets, and one of these was *Madam, will you Walk*. They always dressed in Victorian costumes to perform this; Aunty Win had a long, blue silk dress with a matching parasol. Her wide brimmed cream hat had blue satin ribbons and a veil. She looked very elegant; the dress fitted her slender figure well. Uncle John wore a light grey suit, a white shirt with high wing collar and a silk cravat pinned in the centre, grey waistcoat, long fitted coat and matching trousers, spats and black shoes. The stage was set, their entrance was announced, the music played and the couple came on from opposite sides. "Madam, will you walk? Madam will you talk? Madam, will you walk and talk with me?"

sang the tenor voice, the soprano answered in a similar way, until several verses had been sung. The ending was when the tenor sang "If I give you the keys to my heart, Madam will you walk? Madam, will you talk?" etc. etc. to which she replies "If you give me the keys to your heart, then I *will* walk, etc." All very proper and romantic in true Victorian manner. Lots of applause at the end.

The ladies joined together to sing Gilbert & Sullivan songs such as *"Three Little Maids from School"* and others. The men sang *"As I was going to Strawberry Fair"* and various songs from the Gilbert & Sullivan repertoire. My father joined in and tap-danced; he also played the spoons on one occasion and always sang in the chorus.

Some of the funny comic songs had catchy tunes; people hummed them for days afterwards. There were plenty of opportunities for the audience to join in and sing choruses too. They included little comedy sketches causing plenty of laughter. The Vicar did a few conjuring tricks sometimes, appreciated by the audience especially when they went wrong! There was such a good feeling when the Memorial Hall rang with laughter and applause; customers came into our shop talking about it all and laughing again at funny bits they remembered. It was a wonderful boost to community morale.

OMBERSLEY YOUTH CLUB

Members of Ombersley Youth Club amateur dramatics group took part in a competition run by Worcestershire Youth Clubs circa. 1951 for staging a play. The production they chose entitled *Today of all days* was first performed at Shenstone College, Kidderminster and the Ombersley Youth Club players were competition runners up. All those who took part had been pupils at Ombersley School when I was there, and to this day I remain a friend of Valerie neé Rhodes.

MY FIRST PANTOMIME

When I was six years old Daddy took me to a Christmas pantomime at 25MU Depot, Hartlebury, where he worked. It was the first time I had ever been to a pantomime and I was excited. We got on the Midland Red bus (No.315 to Kidderminster), alighted at "The Talbot" public house and walked down the lane to the huge site of camouflaged buildings. What an adventure it was! I ate lunch with Daddy and the other men and their children in the canteen. I was fascinated to see one man eating all his food by putting it between slices of bread; I had never seen anyone do that before. He put meat, gravy, vegetables everything on his plate, between slices of bread, cut them in half and munched away!

After our meal we walked to the building where the pantomime was being staged. Lights, curtain, prologue; *Cinderella* began; the audience of children with their parents were silent. The cast gave it their all! Men who had never been on stage gave what I thought were wonderful performances as Ugly Sisters, the Fairy Godmother and the Wicked Witch. Young women played Cinderella and Prince Charming; Prince Charming had long shapely legs and a good voice. The wives and families of the cast and other employees had made a massive combined effort to make costumes, construct and paint scenery and to produce the stage, lighting, sound effects and music.

I joined in the fun with the rest of the large audience. We joined in with the songs, laughed until our sides ached and clapped until our hands hurt at the end. I was quiet as we walked to catch the bus back to Ombersley, and on the short journey home. Once I was home I couldn't stop talking, telling Mum all about the pantomime and making her laugh at my descriptions of the funny bits. After supper I went to bed absolutely tired out and fell to sleep quickly remembering the colourful costumes and parts which had appealed to me most. For days afterwards I gave Mum detailed descriptions of pantomime scenes. Then I went through it all again when I was with Grandma; she loved to talk and I could always make her laugh.

GRANDMA'S SENSE OF HUMOUR

I was given a large second-hand tricycle for my birthday, and rode it round to the shop and into the back garden. Grandma admired it, and asked if she could have a go on it! She made us all laugh when she got on and rode it, her knees were enlarged with arthritis and she gathered up her long skirt and pedalled up the garden path. I thought that was hilarious!

BBC RADIO PROGRAMMES

What would people have done without the radio? A range of programmes were broadcast and the service kept going throughout the war years. ITMA (*It's That Man Again*) was a favourite with my parents on Thursday nights between 8.30pm and 9.00pm, broadcast from Bristol. Tommy Handley and some of the funny characters who accompanied him made everyone laugh; Mrs. Mop who always said, "Can I do you now, sir?" always entered the dialogue at the perfect *wrong* moment. Colonel Chinstrap said in reply to most things, "I don't mind if I do", assuming that he was being offered a drink. The show was full of quick witty responses and typically British eccentricities.

Wilfred Pickles, a chirpy Yorkshire chappy, presented *Have A Go,* a light hearted quiz programme with a live audience and cash prizes. People used to remember bits of it and have a laugh in our shop. I enjoyed that programme too when I was old enough to stay up for it. In 1940 *Variety Bandbox* began, which was a music hall programme and had different contributors each week. I remember Ted Ray the comedian, Percy Edwards who whistled and imitated bird song and the singing couple Anne Ziegler and Webster Booth. I am sure that people who remember this programme can add lots of names to that list — I think it was presented by Derek Roy. *Workers Playtime* also became an popular listening; these and various music programmes such as *Music While You Work* could often be heard coming from people's homes in summertime when doors and windows were open. Daddy liked *Sincerely Yours* presented by Vera Lynn, *Desert Island Discs* (1942), and *Forces Favourites*, intended to link men in the forces with their wives and sweethearts; in fact Vera was known as "The Forces Sweetheart".

I was usually at the shop at this time and sat with Grandma who enjoyed *Mrs Dale's Diary* and rarely missed that 4 o'clock programme. It seemed to me that Mrs. Dale said, "I am awfully worried about Jim" in every episode — Jim was the neighbourhood doctor.

I was a devoted listener to *Children's Hour* and enjoyed the regular items contained in it such as *Toy Town* with Uncle Mac, the wonderful Derek McCulloch taking the parts of unforgettable characters such as *Larry the Lamb* and *Dennis the Dachshund*. Larry had a bleating voice and frequently said, "Oh Mr. Mayor Sir!", probably when the irascible *Mr. Grouse* was causing trouble. I loved the Children's Hour series of plays about *Norman and Henry Bones*, the boy detectives who solved all kinds of crimes.

Older children and adults enjoyed *Dick Barton — Special Agent*, who, with his cronies *Jock* and *Snowy*, became involved in very dangerous and exciting situations. That programme began on 7th October 1940 and the series ended in 1950.

BBC RADIO PROGRAMMES

I had to be quiet while Mum listened to *The Brains Trust*; but I listened with total concentration to *The Man In Black* narrated by Valentine Dyall, whose deep velvety, sinister voice led us through these "Appointments with fear" as the detective Dr. Morelle unravelled strange, spooky, mysterious happenings. Excellent stuff for a cold dark night when we could sit around the fire and be mentally transported; our imaginations stimulated by these exciting stories told by such a superb narrator.

Regular "tuning in" to the news and favourite programmes became an important component of the daily routine.

A LITTLE DROP OF WHAT YOU FANCY DOES YOU GOOD! BEER

The village public houses sold beer and all had regular customers, who enjoyed their beer and company in the pubs, but of course those on low incomes couldn't afford to drink very often. The price of beer went up to 1/1d. (one shilling and a penny) a pint in 1940, and the price of whisky rose to 1/9d. for a single measure. Chamberlain's budget put a heavy tax on beer in that year. It was said that when the Americans came they lost no time finding their nearest public houses and encouraged the young girls to drink too much.

THE CIDER BREWERS

Drinking cider was also a social custom, whether sitting down in the fields for a break and a bite to eat, having a laugh and chatting to workmates, or sitting round in someone's cider shed. People enjoyed cider at family gatherings; usually it was consumed when folk relaxed and enjoyed a bit of company. Some farmers kept a cider press and collected all the cider apples and perry pears they could for making cider. For these home brews, the fruit was not cleaned, it was shaken off the trees using long poles and left to ripen on the ground, sometimes it looked as though it was rotting rather than ripening. They didn't pay any attention to the maggots, animal dung and dirt on the fruit, it all went through the scratter to be reduced to pulp for the press. Buckets of pulp were tipped onto big cloths spread out on the base of the press and then folded over the pulp. This process was repeated until there was a pile of cloth parcels, then a wooden board was put on top and the big press was lowered and clamped down until the juice flowed out. That liquid was stored in barrels and when sugar had been added it was allowed to ferment until it was ready for drinking. A farmer who employed six or seven regular hands made 4 hogsheads (a hogshead barrel contains 54 gallons) of cider each year. The men were given a small barrel or stone jar of cider most days to share when they took a break from their work. Farming families and villagers alike had cider in the house for their own use and to offer to visitors.

110

Some country public houses employed a cider maker to make the brew they sold. Villagers, including children, brought bags of windfall apples and pears for pulping and pressing, everyone helped and they brought their small barrels and stone jars to be filled when the brew was ready. There was always plenty left for use in the public house, where it was sold very cheaply. It is said that the fresh cider tasted really good, but for those with a thirst who drank a pint or two, the next day was probably spent making many visits to sitting on the lavatory at the bottom of the garden!

PLUM-JERKUM

Some countrymen made this every year; a man who was both coffin maker and carpenter in a nearby village had a huge barrel he always used for his *special recipe*. Windfall plums, apples and pears were pulped and pressed, and the juice was put into the big open cask. He then added barley, root ginger, pieces of beef and brown sugar. This was left to ferment until a scum formed on top; sometimes they speeded up the fermentation by inserting a hot poker. This created a very potent brew; no wonder the old fellows came to sit in his workshop where the huge barrel of *special brew* stood. I can imagine them there exchanging stories and tasting a horn or two of his delicious plum-jerkum. One year at Christmas time the church choir came round to sing carols, and were invited in for refreshments. They were all given mince pies and small glasses of the plum-jerkum; people who they visited afterwards

111

complained to the Vicar that the lads had been changing the words and *acting the goat!*

TEA IN WORCESTER WITH GRANDMA

In the school holidays and occasionally on Saturdays, Grandma took me on a Midland Red bus to Worcester to do a little shopping and take afternoon tea at one of the cafés. I loved these outings, and enjoyed looking around the shops Grandma went to. I often spent my pocket money on something from Woolworth's. Grandma usually went to a shop called *Whitts* in the High Street, where they sold haberdashery, hats and ladies clothes.

When money was handed over, it was put with the bill into a brass tube, then into the overhead system which sent it rapidly to the cashier. It quickly came hurtling back with the change and a receipt; I found that shop fascinating.

Sometimes we went to The Cadena which stood on the corner of St. Swithin's Street and High Street. The delicious aroma of freshly ground coffee hit one's nostrils as soon as you entered the corner doorway. Opposite was the counter where bread, fresh cakes and pastries were sold; trays of these were displayed in the window by the entrance and the women serving wore smart starched uniforms and caps. The big coffee grinder and shelves containing colourful tins and packets of tea, tins of shortbread biscuits and other Cadena specialities was by the cash desk. The lady in the cash desk had very blonde, carefully waved hair and wore bright red lipstick. Her job was to take all the money for meals served in the upstairs café and the basement restaurant.

As Grandma and I walked upstairs to the café for afternoon tea, we could hear the music from the string quartet usually playing there. Stepping into the carpeted room we would find a table and sit down, I always smiled at the four ladies who were playing, piano, violin, viola and cello. They wore long dresses or skirts in dark rich colours with subtle items of costume jewellery. The viola and violin players placed colourful silk handkerchiefs under their chins when they held their instruments in place to play. The large cellist lady wore spectacles and dangly earrings, and her hair was held in a bun on the back of her head. Their music was a pleasant background for the chatter of customers enjoying tea, and sometimes clapping if a favourite tune was played.

The tablecloths were white and crisply starched, as were the aprons and caps of the waitresses who served us. The tables were laid with plates, cake knives and forks, napkins, cups and saucers, sugar basin and a few fresh flowers in a small china vase. A waitress took the order and quickly returned with a pot of tea and a jug of milk. Grandma liked toasted teacakes or crumpets in cold weather and scones with fresh cream and strawberries when they were in season. Then we had a plate of assorted cakes and pastries brought to the table. I used to look forward to a chocolate éclair or a cream horn, and Grandma liked Battenberg and iced ginger cake.

When we had finished our tea Grandma asked the waitress for a bill and always left her a tip under her plate. We gathered up our parcels, and went downstairs to the cash desk, Grandma passed the bill and some money to the blonde lady, picked up her change and we walked out to make our way to Newport Street to catch the bus back to Ombersley.

CHAPTER
THIRTEEN

The Significant Pig

In Ombersley, a pigsty could be found in many back gardens. I particularly remember those belonging to my relatives in Abberley village too — they had separate accommodation for two pigs, each with a covered sleeping quarter and open walled yard area. These semi-detached pig sties backed onto the rear wall of the family lavatory, a larger than usual convenience which had three wooden seats at different heights, for all family members. Under these wooden seats were buckets to catch all that the family deposited there. One could stroll up the garden path and sit in there on a warm summer day listening to the pigs grunting contentedly and looking through the wide open door at the garden where an apple tree stood. I played with the little girl who lived nearby and we used to sit in the privy together when nature called, watching the birds, butterflies and the cat scratching up the soil. On one such occasion Aunty Ethel was precariously perched on a ladder picking apples from a tree she lost her balance and fell!

Auntie, did you feel no pain,
Falling from that apple tree?
Would you do it, please, again,
'Cos my friend here didn't see?

A rather "uppity" relative once visited my relatives there and returned to the house after a trip to the garden privy saying, "Jack, there is no lock on your lavatory!" "No" he replied "That's right, we haven't had a bucket of s*** stolen yet!"

The pig was an important part of country life, those who kept them knew that they would have plenty of good food for the family when the pig was killed. Feeding the pig cost very little, mash was made using sharps, a bran by-product bulked up with household food waste, windfall apples and garden vegetable waste. I recall seeing boiled "pig potatoes" being taken from an outdoor copper boiler, which were old spuds unsuitable for use as seed, and we picked up small ones and pulled off the skin before eating them. They tasted pretty good to us! When a sow had given birth to a litter, the swill would have "sow and weaner mix" added; this gave the animals added protein and carbohydrates.

Mr. and Mrs. Weeks lived in a cottage close to the back entrance to the buildings belonging to our shop. Mr. Weeks had a brick-built pigsty on his nearby allotment on the other side of Hilltop Lane. My friends and I used to go to the woods and collect bags of acorns to feed to his pig, which were greeted with grunts of delight and much appreciative crunching.

116

Pigs were reared and killed for the meat twice a year, usually in February and October. The pigs were killed at home in those days, and the whole business of slaughtering fascinated me. The weight of domestic pigs when they had reached the time for slaughter was around 300lbs (136kilos). Pigs were always starved for twenty-four hours before being killed; they were given only water. Mr. Weeks always had a friend to help him with the pig slaughter. The pig was led out of the sty on a cord, and Mr. Weeks was ready with his very sharp knife to "stick" it. The knife touched the heart and it was all over. The carcass was wiped with a cloth and warm water to remove any blood. I was laid on a good layer of clean straw belly down, then covered with a layer of loosely shaken straw and set on fire to burn the bristles off. This process was repeated as they turned the pig over until all the bristles had been removed. It was then washed all over with hot water to remove the black residue from the burnt bristles.

Then they tied the dead pig to heavy wooden trestles and the belly was slit open so that all the innards could be removed, together with the liver, lights and veil (or caul) used to wrap faggots. The liver was usually eaten on the same day and no doubt shared with the man who helped at slaughter time. They say that liver from a freshly killed pig or lamb is the finest you can get! All the offal would be quickly used; some would be minced up to make faggots, the stomach lining would be made into tripe, the small intestines would become chitterlings, other bits of meat from the butchering process would be used for sausages. Some villagers

117

used to cure their own bacon and ham, and these joints could be seen hanging in muslin from the kitchen beams.

During the war years, farmers and others who kept pigs had to register with the Ministry of Agriculture for a licence. Inspectors visited each applicant to decide upon the number of animals they could keep. Those who wanted to make extra money, by producing unlicensed pig meat, worked out their own methods for concealing the actual number of animals they reared. The pigs were kept on the move, a few here and a few there; the farmer provided food for the animals, but used ground or premises belonging to relatives, friends and neighbours, until the animals were ready for slaughtering. Then the meat was sold on the black market and those who had been involved in the plan were paid. We had many a laugh at stories of farmers driving around with pigs in their lorries and vans when they knew the Inspectors were around. One man had three gilts in his van and parked in a lane one evening to have a snooze; he had been drinking some very good cider! He slept longer than he intended, the pigs were well settled on the straw, then someone banged loudly on the side of the van, and he woke up with a start! Was it the Inspector? His heart was pounding, night had fallen and he had a lot to answer for. He opened his door and stepped out — imagine his relief when he saw one of his farmhands standing there holding a bicycle!

My grandmother used to make lovely brawn from a pig's head bought from the butcher — his joke was "Shall I leave the eye in, missus, to see you through the week?" This brawn was made by placing the head (cut in half or more pieces according to size required) in a large heavy pan and covered with boiling water, to which she added a bunch of herbs, some onions, salt, pepper and cloves. The meat would be cooked slowly until quite tender and falling off the bone. In another pan some big pieces of shin of beef would also be simmering with onions, turnips, fresh horseradish and seasoning. They tipped into a colander above a bowl to catch the stock. When cool the meat would be taken off the bones, and all fat would be removed. The lean meat from the beef and pork would be coarsely cut into pieces and placed in a bowl, and then freshly ground nutmeg, cayenne pepper, and salt would be added. The cooked meat would be stirred and placed into a large or two small straight-sided earthenware dishes, some of the mixed retained stock would be added, greaseproof paper placed on top and covered with a cloth, then heavy weights would be placed on this to press the meat down. When absolutely cool and set, the brawn was turned out onto a plate and allowed to stand in the cool larder. (It is the skin and bones which give the stock strength to set like a jelly.) The brawn could be cut into slices and served with salad or hot vegetables. It was much enjoyed by men working in the fields, and for picnics, with pickles and crusty bread.

There is no waste from a pig. It is said that the only part which cannot be eaten is its squeal!

CHAPTER
FOURTEEN

Romany Visitors

"Shall we go and see the gypsies?" I asked Anne; she smiled — the idea of going along to talk to them was daring for us. The same Rom or Romany family arrived in Ombersley every year, their brightly painted wooden horse-drawn caravans rolled into our village; word of their arrival quickly went around. These particular Romany visitors always asked permission from Lord Sandys (via his Bailiff) to set up camp in the strip of woodland near to the main road opposite the blacksmith's shop at Sinton. When they set up camp in that place, Anne and I walked across the park and looked over at their caravans; there was always a few of them sitting around the place where they had their fire.

My friend Anne and I usually found out quickly of their arrival, Anne's father was the Bailiff and went to unfasten the gate for them to take their horses and caravans onto that little spot of countryside at the edge of the park where they stayed happily for a few weeks. They travelled in a convoy of three or four horse-drawn wooden caravans, the largest *vardo;* (their Rom word for caravan) belonged to Anna and Tom, it was painted dark red and was very ornate with gilt embellishments and touches of yellow and green here and there to highlight the carving and textured wood around the doors and windows. On the back of the caravan was a cupboard with double doors, where fresh food and a big cooking pot were kept. Beneath the cupboard was a cage for chickens. Their relatives followed on in smaller caravans; two were wooden, also brightly painted and well kept. The fourth was a canvas topped *vardo* belonging to a Rom woman who had two young sons named Wally and Am (possibly short for Abraham) who were good with the horses (gri) and dogs (jeckle). They caught rabbits (coni), wild ducks, and game birds for the pot.

On this warm evening, when we plucked up courage to go and talk to them, the old lady and her husband were sitting near to the fire. They asked us to sit down, we sat on the grass and told them our names. We were nervous but interested; the old man told us he was called Tom by his friends and said, "My Anna here is Queen of the Rom." We began to relax and she took us to see her *vardo*, where there were a lot of brass things inside, and the black iron stove was shining and polished. The top bed at the end was enclosed behind mirrored doors, which had patterns cut into the glass. The lower bed was covered with a brightly coloured rug, and the small windows allowed in just enough light to bring out all the colours of the interior. Anna wore a black skirt and apron with a colourful shawl wrapped around her shoulders, her grey hair was swept away from her brown wrinkled skin and tied back with a red and yellow scarf. She wore lots of gold jewellery and was obviously proud of her splendid *vardo* and her family.

At the fireside, one of the women was lifting what looked like a large stone from the ashes with a shovel. She laid it carefully on the grass, then took a large knife and stabbed it into it, to our surprise it cracked and she cut into it releasing a compact piece of pale steaming meat which gave off a tempting smell, saying "This be edge-pig!" We were fascinated, and they explained that this was a baked hedgehog for their supper. We learned that the way to cook the "edge-pig" is to roll it in soft clay mud and bury it in the hot ashes of a fire to bake. They cut chunks from a large loaf of bread, and everyone had some hedgehog meat to go with it. We were given a little to taste; it tasted good!

My friend Anne had cut her hand on some barbed wire when we were climbing over a fence, and Anna noticed this and looked at the cut. She sent her daughter (who they called "Prinny" because her father said she was his princess) to fetch something; we didn't know what she had asked for because they spoke in Rom between themselves. Prinny came back with a handful of small feathery leaves, which Anna put into a small wooden bowl and crushed with a clean stone. She spread the mixture on Anne's cut telling her to sit still, then she took a large clean leaf to cover the paste, and tied Anne's handkerchief around her hand again. One of the other women came to sit by us and told us that things from the wild were the best medicine.

Prinny went into the caravan and came out with a piece of newspaper; she wanted to show us a picture of

Alb (possibly one of her brothers) who had jumped into a river and saved the life of a child. They couldn't read the printed report but they knew what it was about and were very proud of Alb.

We talked to Prinny and she told us she wanted to meet a dark, handsome Rom lover. She helped her mother to dye the wooden "flowers" which they made by cutting short lengths of wood, removing the bark and shaving thin petal-like slices all around in layers until it resembled a flower; then they soaked them in red, blue and yellow dye, fixed them to thin strong "stalks" and sold them. They also made and sold wooden clothes pegs and some of the women made lace. They *never* begged for money, but they depended mostly on money they could earn from fruit picking, hop picking, potato and root vegetable lifting and any other work on the land. Some of the farmers were glad of their help during the war years when all young men were away from home. As they moved around the country during those years they were never short of agricultural work. Country folk knew that they did a bit of poaching, and helped themselves to some fruit and vegetables when they were working; it was taken for granted that they lived from day to day on what came their way.

When they were lifting swedes, turnips and beet, they were allowed to take some for themselves; it is safe to assume that they took plenty for their horses too. The Rom measured their wealth by their horses. They groomed and attended to them well and ensured that they were properly tethered when necessary. We never saw a Rom horse badly treated or lacking in care; the village farrier was paid to attend to their hooves. Sometimes they paid him with game they had caught, and we heard that once they took him a freshly killed deer; the farrier was always pleased to see them!

The Romany visitors used to come into our shop when they had enough money to buy some food. They asked for bacon scraps from the slicing machine, and broken biscuits. They bought basic ration items and were pleased to get the occasional tin of food if it was offered and they had enough money. The Romanies bought bread from the village baker, and were glad if the butcher would sell them bones and meat scraps. My mother always remembered one of the Rom women with a baby coming into our shop when they were moving on. She asked for a tin of condensed milk "fer me babby" and was short of a halfpenny. Mother said it didn't matter but was assured that they would pay it next time. The following year they returned to the village, and the Romany woman came to the shop and put down the small coin saying "That's what I owes yer."

At Broadwas (a village West of the River Severn, on the A44 road from Worcester leading to Knightwick and Bromyard), people reported the burning of a big Romany caravan. They said it was burnt by the Rom family because the Gypsy Queen had died in it and it was their "law" that her *vardo* should never be used by anyone else.

The general attitude towards them was somewhat negative; they were looked down upon, indeed, some people were not pleased to see them, others were indifferent. Some parents told children to have nothing to do with them. Children found the Romany people fascinating because they were free spirits travelling around the country, speaking their own language and sounding different when they spoke our language. Their way of dress and the stories we heard of their activities appealed to youthful imaginations. We drew pictures of their caravans at school, and talked about them between ourselves; no doubt some of the stories grew like Chinese whispers!

The village publicans would not allow the Romanies into their public bars, so they served them beer and cider to be consumed outside. The local police were always ready to come along when any fights broke out, as was often the case after they had consumed too much drink. That only happened at weekends when they had been paid for casual work on the farms.

Anne and I thought it would be best not to tell our parents of the time we spent at the Romany camp. We kept that experience a secret, but we were glad we got to know them a little; the cut on Anne's hand was clean and healed quickly.

NOTES: ROMANY PEOPLE

I became interested in the Romany people when writing about my own experiences.

I mentioned the Rom grandmother, Hannah Buckland, making a paste of leaves to put on a cut on my friend Anne's hand, this was most likely *Yarrow* leaves, a common wild plant which is known to have antiseptic properties.

The Roms who we knew in Ombersley spoke about a man whose name sounded to us like "Gorjun", and they spoke of him with much laughter, saying things like "he is a slippery one" and "he'll always get out of a tight corner will our Gorjun" . . . I have looked into this and can only guess that the name may have appealed to them due to some vague understanding of the legend of the peasant Gordius and the cutting of the "Gordian Knot" — Shakespeare used it in Henry VI.i.

'Turn him to any cause of policy,
The Gordian Knot of it he will unloose,
Familiar as his garter.'

To cut the Gordian Knot is to get out of a difficult position by one decisive step; to resolve a situation by force or by evasive action.

Romany or gypsy nomadic people used to be thought of as originating in Egypt — hence the name "gypsy" but this is an unfounded theory.

The Rom or Romany language comes from central India, so many of the words can be traced to Hindi. There are a group of Indian nomads who call themselves *Dom*.

	ROM	**HINDI**
house	*kher*	*ghar*
tree	*rukh*	*rukh*
salt	*lon*	*lon*
land	*phuv*	*bhu*
man	*manus*	*manus*
spoon	*roj*	*doi*
black	*kalo*	*kala* in Punjabi
young	*terno*	*tarno*
walk	*ga*	*ja*
sleep	*sov*	*so*
outside	*avri*	*bahir*

The Rom language went through a process of transformation as Romany people travelled in Europe — Soravia says "It is a rich and flexible language, with complex declensions for nouns and verb conjugations which allow for a very wide degree of communication."

The Anglo Romani people surviving, speak a mixture of English and Romani. Welsh Romani is now extinct.

The *Buckland* Rom family to whom I refer are on record dating back to Lementine Buckland of 1821 who was then known to visit Chaddesley Corbett in Worcestershire.

There are many other Rom families who were known in this area during the 19th century.

CHAPTER
FIFTEEN

Tell Me a Story

During WWII when I was growing up, when folk had time to rest they sat and talked, often exchanging old stories of family experiences where remembered. The teapot was right there at the centre of the known universe, sometimes glasses of homemade wine or cider were brought out. Throughout my life I have often heard people say "I remember people in our family telling us all kinds of stories about experiences of people in the village; I wish I had written them down." So much has been lost, never to be passed on; after all it is part of the history of the lives of ordinary folk in a bygone era.

RECALLING CHILDHOOD CONVERSATIONS WITH MY GRANDMOTHER — NÉE ANNIE QUARTERMAN, BORN 1872 DAUGHTER OF GEORGE & MARY QUARTERMAN, ABBERLEY WORCS

I always enjoyed sitting quietly with Grandma listening to stories of when she was young in Abberley. She was one of twelve children and had so many tales to tell about life with her parents and brothers and sisters at Brookend Farm and at Manchester House, their shop. When her parents bought Manchester House, and set up their general stores business there, her elder brother John took over the farm and remained there to run it alone. This coincided with her return from Switzerland where she had been attending a "finishing school". She had been taught how to cook, sew, wash, clean and look after farm animals at home; her parents considered she was now ready to do that job. She made friends with the wife of a neighbouring farmer and was not too far away from her parents and brothers and sisters who lived at the shop. She worked hard, loved the country life and enjoyed helping her unmarried brother at the farm for over four years. She met my Grandfather, John William Pester, a year before their marriage on 23rd January 1895. After that her life really changed; she moved to live in West Bromwich, lived at his shop, had five children and worked very hard indeed.

HAM FOR SUPPER

When Grandma was a schoolgirl, she was helping her older sister Alice in the kitchen one day; their mother had told them to cut some ham for the evening meal. Grandma described their large farm kitchen with the big table standing in the middle where most family meals were eaten. Alice decided the big home-cured ham hanging from a hook in the beam above the table was too large and heavy to take down, so, after sharpening the ham knife she got up onto the table and took the muslin off the ham. Then Gran passed up the sharp knife and she began slicing, and handing the slices down onto the plate. Suddenly, the knife stuck a little, so she increased the pressure and brought the blade straight through also taking off the tip of her nose! Alice yelled and climbed down, blood poured, Grandma picked up the nose tip from the floor where it had fallen, and dipped it in fresh water. Alice immediately pressed the bit of flesh back onto her nose and continued to keep her fingers on it for some time; it stopped bleeding, and remained in place eventually leaving only a hairline scar, which faded with time.

THE DANCING BEAR

"Quick, quick, he's coming!" I called, trying to get my sisters and brothers to follow me up the road towards the sound of a hand bell clanging. I knew that sound, it was a signal that the man with the dancing bear was arriving. We all ran up the road panting towards the sound, and he appeared over the brow of the hill; a big man with rich brown curly hair settling on his collar. He wore a large wide brimmed hat, well-worn like the rest of his clothes, his heavy coat had certainly seen better days as had his crumpled trousers and dirty boots. He had a canvas bag on his back and held the end of the chain joined to the big collar around the bear's neck. It was a great brown bear with a thick matted coat and it ambled along by its owner. We walked with him to the place where he had stopped before at the road junction. The bear man sat on the milestone pulling a bottle from his bag and taking a long swig, then he got a piece of bread from his pocket and took out some cheese wrapped in a grubby handkerchief, cutting pieces off it with a pocket knife, he ate them with the bread. The bear flopped down on the grass. They walked all day stopping at villages to entertain and earn a little money. We offered to bring water for the bear, and brother Jack and I went to get it from the pump at the back of our house. I ran inside and asked Mother if she had anything we could take for the bear to eat, and she handed me some stale bread and told me to take some apples from a bucket on the stable floor.

Gradually people began to gather around them. The man had rested and finished his food, and the bear seemed to be thirsty, so we refilled his water bucket and he crunched on the apples. Then the man tied a rope to the end of the bear's chain and took a small fiddle from his bag. Taking off his hat and placing it on the ground, he stood with the instrument tucked under his chin and began to play a tune. The bear stood on his hind legs and began to move around, lifting his feet in tune to the music. Our friends and neighbours were enjoying the foreign sounding tunes which the bear man played, and enjoyed seeing the great animal do its dance. They threw coins into the man's hat and encouraged him to play more tunes. This was a rare event in our village, I only saw the dancing bear twice.

THE GYTRASH

There it was again, footsteps coming behind me, I was scared but when I looked round there was no one there. I was thinking about the party I had just left, it was my brother Robert's birthday and we all enjoyed ourselves. Now I was walking back home to the farm and it was becoming dark as clouds covered the moon. I was sure I was being followed, but I kept going, thinking it's not far now. I had turned off the main road into the lane to the farm, just a cart track with a hedge and some trees on either side. Then roosting birds flew out of a tree behind me. Startled, I turned around again just as the clouds moved and the moonlight came through the trees and lit up the track, and there was something white coming towards me! It really frightened me, I began to quicken my pace, I couldn't run because I was carrying a heavy basket. I looked over my shoulder, there it was again, following me. I didn't dare to look around again but kept walking on as quickly as I could. It was such a relief when I got near to the gate leading to the garden path at the front of the farmhouse. The door was open and I called out, my brother John stepped out to meet me, I put the basket down and gasped that I was being followed by something white. We went to the gate together to look, and there in the middle of the lane stood a small white pony! I remained where I stood, John walked towards it, then a strange thing happened — the pony turned around and disappeared. "My God!" said John, "it was a Gytrash!" Folk in our part of the country used that word to describe sightings of a horse or dog in spirit form. There were several such stories in those days; a black dog dragging a chain had been seen in much the same way.

THUNDERSTORM

Another story Grandma told me many times was about the thunderstorm. She was rearing some ducklings and had set up a pen for them in a meadow near the farmhouse. It was a hot day, there had been rumblings of thunder and the clouds above were dark and heavy. The rain started and she ran up the field to put her ducklings safely under cover. Before she got to them, there was an almighty thunder clap and the skies opened. Rain was pelting down and the lightning flashed and as she ran it struck the pen, and a burning ball dropped to the ground. She turned on her heels and ran as fast as she could back down the field. Hearing the sizzle of the flaming ball rolling down behind her, she flew up the path and into the house. She gasped out her account of what had happened to her brother who was sceptical. They stood and watched the storm subside, then went out to inspect the ducklings.

There, just by the gate was a large, round, solid dark ball of something still steaming hot! They retraced the singed path it had made as it rolled down the slope from the duckling pen, and found several little dead ducklings. Grandma said this must have been a thunderbolt. Lots of people came to look at it (it may still be there). After that she was always very frightened of thunder, and at Ombersley she went to sit in the cupboard under the stairs during a thunderstorm.

HAYMAKING

When hay-making time came around at Brookend Farm, Gran was busy baking extra bread and making cakes to take into the fields at tea-time. She asked the carter's wife to help her carry it all out to the men; they would all sit around smelling the sweet dry hay and enjoy a good tea. I can just imagine her there with the men, shirtsleeves rolled up and faces bronzed by the sun. She would spread a cloth on the ground and spread out trays of freshly cut crusty bread, home made butter and jam, scones, cake and cheese. She made lemonade for them to drink, which they needed plenty of to quench their thirst. When the last load had been taken to the rick and it was finished, her brother sometimes took out some cider.

LAMB-TAILING

At the end of the lambing season she went out to lend a hand with "lamb tailing". Her brother removed the lambs' tails, and she used to sit on a board and hold each lamb as he cut the tail off quickly with a red-hot iron. She said that didn't seem to bother them, it was done very quickly. She always had a pot of water boiling on a wood fire nearby, and as soon as a tail was cut, a loop of string was tied on it and it was held in the boiling water for a short time. This made it easy to pull off the wool. Some of the early lambs had quite big tails, which were quite a delicacy. She made lamb's tail pie and her brother also liked the tails dipped in beaten egg and fried.

REYNARD THE CUNNING ONE

John Quarterman had two dogs, *Nipper* the terrier and *Danny* the lurcher. He was out shooting one day with two friends, when the dogs got the scent of a fox, and began to run following its trail. The fox appeared chasing a rabbit. The dogs joined the chase and the lurcher caught the fox. *Nipper* wasn't far behind and joined in, barking and snarling. When John reached the spot the fox was lying there, left for dead. The dogs had gone off after the more tasty rabbit meat. He picked the fox up by its hind legs, dropped it by a gate and walked on; his friends following behind, saw him do this and just as they approached the gate the fox stood up, looked around and ran off. John was very surprised and they all thought it unusual because they were sure the dogs had killed it. Grandma said that is one of the ways a fox can show its cunning; he can pretend to be dead when it suits him! Country folk used to say that a fox can stare a pheasant or other bird down from a tree. It will look at the bird, and walk round and round the tree continuing to look up when it passes below. The bird watches the fox, becomes dizzy and falls off the branch; a lightning pounce ensures its rapid death — Reynard the cunning one!

GRANDMA'S 21ST BIRTHDAY

The following is a story I never tired of hearing and used to ask Grandma to tell it to me again and again. She would laugh, make a pot of tea, we would make ourselves comfortable and then she would begin . . .

"My 21st birthday was in 1894, my parents always arranged a special party for each of us when we 'came of age'. My parents had been discussing what they would organise for me, when the invitation came along from the Earl and Countess of Dudley for them to attend a ball at Witley Court in the Autumn of that year. It happened like this: the Countess came into the shop with a large order and Father thanked her for the invitation she handed to him, adding that it coincided with my 21st birthday. She immediately said the invitation would include me; she didn't forget, a printed invitation arrived with my name on it. The Dudleys had invited some very important guests to Witley Court for a week. They had organised a shooting party, riding, and other activities, culminating in a grand ball arranged for the last night. I was very excited about this, but also wanted to celebrate my birthday with our family. So I invited Mother and Father to tea at the farm with my brother John and me. Most of our brothers and sisters came too bringing gifts and cards for me. Mother and Father gave me a beautiful engraved gold fob watch and I received some very nice presents and cards from our relations and friends.

"Plans were made for Mother to take me to the dressmaker, which was an important event as we all had to be correctly dressed. Mother looked splendid in her ball gown, made for a previous occasion, Father had his evening dress. Mother asked Kitty, the dressmaker, to come to the shop to take my measurements and show us designs for ball gowns. She suggested the one I chose should be made in taffeta silk and wrote out the quantities of fabric, lining and petticoat material, ribbon, lace and bindings required. The next day John drove me to the shop. Mother was ready, Father had had the horse and trap waiting in the yard, he drove us to Worcester. Mother and I went to a shop and sat on chairs by the counter. Smartly dressed assistants brought materials in a range of lovely colours; it was hard to choose. I loved the shot silks, especially the palest blue one. Mother agreed with my colour choice and it was the taffeta weave our dressmaker suggested. We handed over Kitty's list and we were shown suitable linings and petticoats, the other things we needed.

"The fabrics were measured and cut according to Kitty's instructions, we took it all to her house on our way home. She said she would start on the gown straight away and let us know when she wanted me for my first fitting; several fittings followed until the gown was finished in good time for the ball. It fitted me well, the petticoats with lace edging gave the skirt fullness and the tightly fitting bodice and waist suited my figure. I piled my long hair up on top of my head, and pinned it securely, adding a comb to which Kitty had added a delicate decoration made from my dress fabric. The neckline was low, and the gown had short puffed sleeves. I wore long cream kid gloves and matching shoes."

"Witley Court was glittering with light and we could hear music when the coachman took our carriage away at the front of the house. Inside it was so beautiful, the chandeliers glistened, great bowls of fresh flowers were everywhere, it quite took my breath away. We followed other guests to the ballroom where our cards were handed to their Master of Ceremonies who announced everyone by name, then we shook hands with the Earl and Countess of Dudley and walked into the great ballroom. The evening was just wonderful, the Prince of Wales was there and the Earl and Countess of Cadogan, the Duke and Duchess of Devonshire and numerous other noble and titled guests. I had a dance card, and there was no shortage of gentlemen who asked me to dance and put their names on my card. I had a wonderful evening and my parents enjoyed it too, saying that the cold buffet was superb and the musicians and vocalists were very good. The Prince danced with some beautiful ladies, he seemed to be really enjoying himself. Mother told me that one of the beautiful ladies was probably his mistress. It was a fairytale experience for me, like being in a palace."

I used to try to draw pictures of Grandma in her ball gown and colour them in with my crayons — she laughed when she saw my efforts, so I used to put in things like a mouse peeping out under her skirt, or a bird on her head. Our laughter could sometimes be heard in the shop, and Mum and Aunty Win came to see what it was all about!

A STORY FROM GRANDMA'S DAYS IN WEST BROMWICH

Grandma loved the countryside, especially Abberley and the lush meadows, hedges and hillside woodlands. She always said she missed it very much when she married and went to live in West Bromwich.

"O England, country of my heart's desire,
Land of the hedgerow and the village spire,
Land of thatched cottages and murmuring bees,

Your swallows 'neath the eaves, your sweet
   content!
And 'mid the fleecy clouds that o'er you spread,
Listen, the skylark singing overhead . . .
That's the old country, that's the old home!
You never forget it wherever you roam.

From a poem "The Old Country"
by E.V. Lucas 1868–1939

"Your Grandpa used to keep big carthorses in those days. He had two named Dash and Carlo, who sometimes pulled the big heavily loaded cart together. One winter Dash fell and suffered a bad leg injury. He had a friend who bred and understood horses, who was consulted and said Dash should be shot. Grandpa wouldn't hear of it, he loved his horses. So Dash was taken to his stable, where they lifted him up (just so his hooves were off the floor) with big straps attached to a

139

beam. His wound was cleaned and cauterised, splints were made to support the break and bandaged in place. There he remained, suspended receiving careful attention; he had the company of Carlo at the end of each day. The injured leg healed and he was gradually put to work again using the smaller cart and lighter loads — quite an achievement in those far-off days!'

OMBERSLEY WAS A PLACE FOR MANY SMALL BUSINESSES

Grandma told me that when they first arrived in Ombersley, villagers told them that there had formerly been plenty of businesses in the village. There were three blacksmiths, though we only ever knew of the one at the corner of Sinton Lane. There had been a cooper there too and a shoemaker — we only had Mr. Sanders who did the snobbing. There had been several grocery shops, bakeries, clothing shops, and little cottage shops offering all kinds of goods.

The story Grandma liked was the one about the clothing shop on the opposite side of the road to their shop. (It was close to the churchyard and later named *Grafton House*, occupied by a family named Edwards when I lived there.) That shop was called *Tommy Rotten's Cottons* and the man who ran it was known for his stock of cotton clothing. He sold hard-wearing working trousers made of fustian and corduroy. He had good shirts in dimity (cotton fabric woven with raised stripes) and bolts of calico, muslin and other cotton fabrics. He was widely remembered for the notice in his window saying:

Come early in the morning — trousers are coming down."

TRAVELLERS CAME TO OMBERSLEY

Grandpa and Grandma remembered stage coaches from their younger days. They discovered that Ombersley was a place where stage coaches used to stop. They were told that people were frequently put down and picked up by stage coaches in the village in the days when coaches were called *The Everlasting, The Bang-up* and *The Victoria*. In the early days of the 19th century, travellers came to the village by horseback and on horse-drawn vehicles along the old pack road which brought them to the old village cross where the market was held. No doubt these coaches continued to arrive in the village until the advent of motor vehicles.

CHAPTER
SIXTEEN

Wartime Memories

News of the Coventry bombing and the shock of the extent of that attack left people nervous when bombers flew overhead. The engines of German bombers sounded different to those of British planes. Many people remember seeing the sky lit up at night after the bombing raids on Coventry and Birmingham. In Worcester, the *Meco* (Mining Engineering Company) factory in St. John's was bombed.

Enemy aircraft returning to Germany after attacks upon Birmingham and Coventry discharged their remaining bombs at random. Local people said that British "Tiger Moth" aeroplanes being used for training at Peridswell in Worcester used to land in a field at Grimley near Top Barn Farm.

The pilot of a German plane spotted them coming down. The Dutch barns belonging to the farm looked like hangars from the air, and three bombs were dropped on them and they went up in flames. Houses in that area had been painted with camouflage colours, and villagers said that pilots of German aircraft could easily have mistaken this area for an airfield. Three more bombs were also dropped on the road between

Grimley village and Holt. Bombs fell on the Harry Cheshire School in Kidderminster, and at Broughton Hackett. Several incendiary bombs fell on Ashchurch, near Tewkesbury, Glos. A German aircraft crashed on the railway line in Wychbold, near Droitwich. Reports reached us of aircraft crashes in Shropshire. Railway lines were targeted — several bombs fell on or near the railway lines at Bredon's Norton and Eckington.

Lord Sandys has confirmed that Hitler had plans to use Ombersley Court as the German Army Head Quarters for their attack on Birmingham. In the village a Royal Observer Corps post was set up in a field about a quarter of a mile from the school. The Chief Observer was Mr. Laurie Humphries, assisted by several volunteers. It was equipped with a searchlight for spotting and tracking enemy aircraft heading for Birmingham and Coventry, and a telephone.

The small town of Droitwich Spa lies only three miles away from Ombersley; it took on a most important role during the war years. Four of the large hotels there were commandeered to house military and Government personnel. Officer Cadet Training Units, Auxiliary Territorial Service (ATS), Signals and the Royal Army Pay Corps were also there. Scores of civil servants from main cities were evacuated and billeted in Droitwich. Canadian Red Cross nurses were there too.

Westwood Park, a 16th century hunting lodge with extensive grounds and lake near to Droitwich, was used as a camp for large numbers of American soldiers. For them it became a staging post and an important centre for their support operations. Ombersley families invited

143

American servicemen to tea on Sunday afternoons. Those wishing to do so had to register an official request at the village Post Office.

There was a big German Prisoner of War camp at nearby Hampton Lovett, and another camp for Italian Prisoners of War was also based in the area. The prisoners were mostly employed on farms in the area; Italian prisoners were often given accommodation on the farms employing them.

The Home Guard took on responsibility to keep watch on public buildings, roads, railways, waterways and coasts; they kept a sharp lookout for enemy invaders, who may have arrived by parachute and unauthorised coastal landings. Many enemy airmen who had baled out of aircraft were brought in.

There was no shortage of experienced ex-officers and qualified men to take on the responsibility of running the Ombersley District Home Guard; throughout the war years they maintained a group of over forty unpaid volunteers aged between 16 and 65. Some were equipped with rifles, but other men had to use sporting guns. The lack of equipment in the early days of the war resulted in some men using golf clubs, walking sticks and broom handles.

The Ombersley and District Home Guard maintained a post by the bridge over the River Severn at Holt Fleet. One night a man began crossing the bridge and was challenged in the usual way. He obviously had no respect for the Home Guard. He refused to respond, even when the challenge was repeated at bayonet point. His journey and his life ended there, he was buried in

Holt churchyard where his grave can be seen. On another occasion footsteps were heard coming through the fog, the challenge was called, repeated and finally the dark shape was fired at. Then it became clear that they had shot a particularly productive and treasured cow!

For us children life went on, though we were aware that Britain was at war with Germany, and had constant reminders. Our parents and village people were very apprehensive, as some people were worried about relatives and village men involved in the action. However, we didn't suffer the frightening, harrowing experiences of those living in big cities and other parts of the country. We always had enough to eat; ours was a food producing area and so rationing didn't cause villagers as much hardship as it did for those in urban areas. Some villagers were really poor, but they managed to get by somehow; help always came from somewhere when it was needed.

From Ombersley 180 men were called up to serve in WW2; nine of them did not return — all killed in action.

PART TWO:

VILLAGE PEOPLE

CHAPTER
SEVENTEEN

The Vicar of Our Parish

REV. GEORGE GILLINGHAM — JULY 1949

The Rev. George Gillingham was our Vicar; he was always at the centre of village life. I remember him as a small man with a round lined face and thinning hair. He took regular Sunday services, and attended to funerals, marriages, christenings, special services and confirmation classes for the children. He attended numerous Parish Council meetings and meetings of other groups and associations. He was of course a Governor for Ombersley Endowed School, and as such visited the school at intervals throughout the year.

Rev. Gillingham endeavoured to take part in village life as much as possible. He often made home visits, sometimes walking to see parishioners who were incapacitated or dying. He was a good sport and took an active part in village cricket proving to be a good player, and showed a keen interest in all other sporting activities. He had a sense of humour and had learned to do some conjuring tricks, which raised a laugh at village concerts and other occasions, especially when he got them wrong!

The Vicar and his wife had no children and lived in the Old Rectory, a large 18th century house in the centre of the village. The lawn at the front was used as a tennis court and those who enjoyed a game were welcome to use it. Even my friends and I were allowed to play on it at times, using borrowed racquets and having a very rudimentary grasp of the rules of the game. It was probably the only tennis court in the village in those days.

Mrs. Gillingham came from a well-off family and had a private income, a welcome supplement to the Vicar's stipend. She was always very smartly dressed and ladylike — I was told that she had been educated at a private boarding school and had been sent to a "finishing school" before she was married. Her deportment and knowledge of household management certainly showed evidence of her education and parental guidance.

The Gillinghams employed two single unrelated women, both of whom lived at the Old Rectory. They were called Daisy and Lucy and were said to have come from an orphanage; perhaps the Gillinghams took them in when they first set up home together. Mrs. Gillingham arranged their training; she told my grandmother that she took them both to work with the staff at her parents' home to begin with, then continued instructing them herself. Daisy was the housekeeper and cook and Lucy acted as maid, general household helper and cleaner.

Daisy and Lucy were both quiet well-mannered women. Daisy was obviously the more intelligent of the two, and she fitted into the role of companion and lady's maid to Mrs. Gillingham. Lucy was somewhat shy and her hands certainly bore evidence of the hard work she did in and around the house. Lucy was well spoken and enjoyed having an evening off to go to dances in the Village.

They had visitors at the Old Rectory — sometimes a couple who had lived overseas for many years. The man was small and thin with a wrinkled, brown face, who came into the shop asking for "Monkey Brand" soap. This was grey gritty soap made for cleaning very dirty hands. He said he had never tried it before coming to Ombersley, and was finding it very good for his skin, using it in the bath! He bought several bars, much to the amusement of my mother and aunt who said it wouldn't improve his wrinkles!

On Sundays Mrs. Gillingham, Daisy and Lucy could be seen in the front left-hand pew in the 19th century church of St. Andrew. They rarely missed a Sunday, always quiet and dignified dressed in their Sunday best clothes, attentively participating in the services. My grandmother regularly occupied a pew further down the aisle, and sometimes talked to Mrs. Gillingham outside the church after a service. She always told us what they had been talking about when we were having our Sunday dinner. She was occasionally invited to take afternoon tea at The Old Rectory.

Returning from one of those visits, she told me they had talked about jewellery, because they had each admired items worn by the other. On that occasion Mrs. Gillingham sent Daisy to bring down her jewellery

151

box and she showed all her lovely pieces of gold and precious stones to Grandma. As soon as she returned home Gran sat down and told me all about it, describing some items in detail. She had thoroughly enjoyed her afternoon out at the rectory.

Apart from very occasional visits to our shop and church services, Mrs. Gillingham didn't seek much contact with the villagers; no doubt she considered that to be her husband's duty. She took an interest in the garden and gave instructions to anyone they employed to attend to the shrubs, trees, lawn, rockeries and kitchen garden.

There was a large orchard at the rear of the vicarage where a mixture of fruit trees yielded an annual harvest. A man scythed down the long grass before the fruit was picked. They came into our shop to buy vinegar for the pickles and chutneys and sugar for the sweet preserves. Daisy and Lucy made the jams, chutneys and pickles, Mrs. Gillingham wrote the labels and stuck them on the jars. They kept chickens in a run near to the back door and always had enough eggs for their own use.

The Gillinghams entertained modestly and were invited to dine with their friends in return. I remember Lucy coming into our shop once to collect a large joint of ham we had ordered for her from Marsh & Baxters. Lucy told my mother that they were having people in for dinner and Rev. Gillingham was particularly fond of baked ham. She said she always baked ham in a flour and water paste to keep in the flavour and juices. They led a comfortable, quiet lifestyle.

CHAPTER
EIGHTEEN

Wilfred John Dyson
1909–1987

BETTER KNOWN AS "WILF" DYSON — CHURCH VERGER AND SCHOOL CARETAKER

Wilf was always at the forefront of village life, a man of strength and energy. His jobs as verger, sexton and caretaker for St. Andrew's church, and caretaker for the village school kept him in regular contact with the villagers. He opened up the church for services, attended to the heating and ventilation, and was around when the congregation arrived and departed. Church services were supported by his strong voice from the back pew reserved for him and his family. He wound the church clock twice a week without fail. There was a gravedigger, I cannot remember his name, and when he was unavailable Wilf took over. His attention to the matter of keeping the church sufficiently heated when the weather was cold should not be overlooked.

Wilf and his wife Winny had two sons, Roy and Terry and they lived in a small cottage attached to the northern wall of our shop and house. They had a large garden behind that cottage with apple trees and a pigsty. I remember playing with their son Terry who was in my class at school. One day when I was there with him, Mrs. Dyson was taking hot potatoes cooked in their skins out of the big coal-fired boiler by the back door. These were old sprouting spuds cooked up for the pig. She laid them on a sack to cool and we gingerly picked up a spud each, blowing on our fingers as we pulled away the skin and bit into the soft creamy body of the spud; they tasted good! After the war ended they moved from that cottage to "Verger's Cottage" in Church Lane next to the garage, (now known as "Church Cottage") which had been occupied by Miss Smith the schoolteacher. Both homes were very close the church.

Mr. and Mrs. Dyson took care of the church inside and out, and Winny ensured that ladies of the village who were on the cleaning rota kept it up to scratch — I am sure she did her share too. Village ladies took care of providing and arranging flowers for the church. Wilf did as much as he was able to keep the large churchyard reasonably tidy. It did become somewhat overgrown in parts, but he attended to the drive, main pathways and grass verges. Other people were brought in to attend to the trees around the church. Wilf opened up the church and was in attendance for all ceremonies and services held there. He held keys for the Church Room and the Sandys family Mausoleum standing in the churchyard. Wilf's cheery personality and robust appearance were reassuring to people, as he exuded a feeling that all was well in our little corner of the country.

School caretaker was Wilf's other job, and he could be seen pedalling his way to and from the village school on his big sturdy black bike. In the winter he had fires to attend to in all the classrooms. Ashes had to be cleared at the end of the day, fires laid with newspaper and wood and coal buckets to be filled in each classroom. Then there were the lavatories to be dealt with.

Wilf ensured that the classrooms were cleaned (he had help with that), that all windows and doors were secured at the end of each day, and attended to the general maintenance of the buildings. He swept the playground areas, cleared away snow and spread salt and grit on pathways when the surface was frozen, paying particular attention to "slides" we children made when there was snow to play in, and put salt and grit on them too — spoilsport! He always had an eye for our safety and did anything he could to prevent us from injury.

What would we have done without Wilf?

This brief picture of a good, dependable, honest man who always did his best for everyone and worked hard during the war years and throughout his life, is but a small tribute to Wilf and many like him who were the backbone of our country.

CHAPTER
NINETEEN

Turnmill and the Bull Family

Turnmill is quite a romantic place with a long and interesting history. It used to be called *Tirl Mill*, when the big mill was in action and the miller took grain from farms in the wider Ombersley area. All that remains of the actual mill is the brick lined cavity where the great wheel was originally located on the opposite side of the lane near the lake.

To me it seemed that Mr. and Mrs. Bull and their family had always been there at Turnmill House. I discovered later that they arrived in the village from Birmingham as soon as it became certain Britain was on the brink of the Second World War. Throughout the war years Mr. Bull and his sons Peter and Derek drove to and from the Birmingham area to their business. I am unsure what their trade was; did they have a butcher's shop? Or was it something associated with building? Mr. and Mrs. Bull had three sons, Charles was the eldest, then Peter and Derek was youngest. They had a young woman, Kate, who I understood they had either adopted or taken in — she was fit and healthy but had what would now be identified as *Downs Syndrome*. Kate was company for Mrs. Bull while her husband and sons were away from home and she helped with the household chores. I think Charles Bull — always known as "Chuck" — was called up at the beginning of the war, and I remember him being around after the end of the war.

Mrs. Bull used to walk to our shop, for much of the year she could use the path around the side of the lake and into the Ombersley Court Park, crossing the road opposite Sinton Lane and walking up into the village. She carried a big basket and Kate carried a homemade shopping bag. They usually sat on the bentwood chairs standing in the centre of our shop next to the counters. Mrs. Bull talked to my Aunty Win and my mother and was happy for them to serve other customers while she had a bit of a rest. The shop was always a place for conversation, where people shared local "news", their dialogue covering a diverse range of topics, sometimes disagreeing, sometimes laughing, always lively.

Occasionally Mrs. Bull and Kate took the bus to Worcester. It must have been quite a treat for them to take a shopping trip and have tea or a meal at the British Restaurant in the Cornmarket, where they could have a lunch for one shilling.

Mrs. Bull invited my mother and me for tea one day; we walked across the Park and noticed swans and moorhens swimming on the lake. When we arrived at Turnmill House we climbed the six or seven steps to the gate, where there was a hand pump on the left at the top of the steps. The scent of lavender met us, great

157

bushes of it were by the gate and elsewhere as we stepped into the garden where I recall flowering plants and trees near to the front of the house. The lilacs were in blossom, mauve and white, and I remember pink flowering currant there too — I always thought that shrub smelled like cats' pee!

The brick pathway running along the front of the house had bits of aubrieta spilling over the edge. Mrs. Bull came to the open kitchen door and we followed her inside; a tabby cat passed us on its way out. The stone floor was bare save for a homemade rag rug lying close to the hearth in front of a large old black-leaded, cast iron range with a mantelpiece above. An oblong scrubbed table and wooden chairs stood in the middle of the room and a high backed wooden Windsor arm chair faced us, another cat contentedly sleeping on the cushion. There was a big sink and wooden draining board beneath the window. They must have had an electrically operated water-pump, I remember seeing a tap over the kitchen sink. There was not much light in that room as the window was small.

Mrs. Bull was talking to Mum and I went back into the garden to stroke their friendly dog basking in the sunshine. Then we went into the living room, where tea was laid on the table on a starched hand embroidered tablecloth. My mother admired the cloth and Mrs. Bull said she made it, then she talked about embroidery and showed us other things she had made. She certainly was an accomplished needlewoman, her work was beautiful. Mum had lived in West Bromwich for the earlier part of her life, and knew Castle Bromwich and other suburbs of Birmingham, so they found plenty to talk about. I asked if I could leave the table and look out of the window at the rear of the room; the view through the treetops and down the tree lined bank to the brook flowing towards the river attracted my attention. I thought it would be wonderful to live in a house with a view like that. I am sure the Bull family were very happy that they had found such a little paradise in which to spend those war years.

Mrs. Bull showed us some photographs of their Birmingham home and the boys when they were little. I asked her why they called their eldest son "Chuck" and she made me smile telling us that when he was a baby, she could always stop him crying by bouncing him on her knee and singing "Charley, Charley, Chuck Chuck Chuck" which made him chuckle! The name stuck.

We didn't see any more of the inside of the house than that; it seemed a long house with many windows and two doors on the front facing the garden. I cannot remember whether there was a porch over the front door or not; it may have opened into a hallway with the staircase. I can only guess.

On another day, I walked to Turnmill with my father. Peter Bull was clearing debris from the sluice gate where water from the lake poured down, passing through a tunnel under the lane and winding its way down to the River Severn. The old stone structure around the "waterfall" and sluice was kept clear of weeds, Mr. Bull and his sons took care of that. We spoke to Peter and then went up towards the shed where they had their electric generator, Mr. Bull was

159

doing something to it at the time, and was very pleased that it responded immediately when he started it up.

Three rabbits hung from their hind legs beneath the roof. Mr. Bull said he shot them the previous day and they were all looking forward to some rabbit stew. No doubt they also shot pheasants and wild ducks around there too. Daddy talked to him about fishing as the Bull boys and their father enjoyed fishing in the river. Daddy talked about his fishing and camping experiences in Brittany and Mr. Bull said he and the boys enjoyed coarse fishing there and caught a variety of fish such as eels, dace, pike, chub, bream, gudgeon and roach. They knew someone who caught a big salmon by the weir at Holt Fleet, and trout had been caught there too. Mr. Bull said how strong the current is on that stretch of the river and they spoke of accidents and even deaths by drowning in the stretch up to Holt Fleet.

He took us to another shed where he showed us a litter of puppies with their mother. He said they would have no difficulty finding customers for them; the were brown and white mongrels (possibly a spaniel/terrier cross).

When I was a toddler, Mum used to go for long walks with me in an old black perambulator; this four-wheeled carriage had a removable section in the middle of the interior. When I was learning to walk this was removed so that I could ride in a full sitting position. I walked a little and rode a little and Mother explored all the lanes around the village. The bumpy lane to Turnmill was a favourite when the ground was dry, though in wet weather it was punctuated with puddles, some quite deep. Families and courting couples visited Turnmill when the weather was fine.

On the 10th July 1942 I had my fifth birthday party picnic in a field down Turnmill Lane; Janet and Susan Wood, Pat Singleton and Rosemary Spragg were invited. The Wood sisters and Pat came to our house, and Rosemary Spragg walked up from Holt Fleet and met us at the top of the lane. Mum put all the food, plates, cups, kettle, primus stove and a cloth into the old pram and trundled it down the lane, until we got to the gate leading to a field almost opposite the old barn, which stood on the left of the lane leading down to the place where the old mill wheel stood. Mum opened the gate and pushed the old pram into the field as far as she could before the fall of the ground became a bit tricky.

The field sloped quite steeply at the end, on the right was a coppice and on the left at the bottom of the slope the stream bubbled along on its way to the River Severn. That field was a really good place for children with all sorts of places for hide and seek, the brook to paddle in, and at that time it was covered with mole hills. We had great fun jumping from one to another and just playing around in that green field, making daisy chains, and holding buttercups under chins to test whether we liked butter!

Mum spread the cloth on the ground and put out sandwiches, little cakes and biscuits. She set up the primus stove and put the kettle on to boil so she could make tea. We all had a great time.

One winter we had snow and a period of hard frosts. The ground froze, and we had ice on our windows when we awoke in the mornings. It was very pretty when the curtains were drawn and the morning light shone through. (I used to snuggle down in my warm bed as the bedrooms were cold, and I was allowed to bring my clothes down and dress by the fire in a warm room, both at the shop and at the cottage.) We soon heard that the lake was frozen hard; I couldn't wait to go down to Turnmill and see for myself. I called for Anne and we went down there together. The lane was frozen and the ruts where puddles formed were patches of hard ice, it looked promising! When we reached the lake we found young lads having a great time sliding on the ice. We gingerly got over the low wall and tried it for ourselves. Then other people arrived including Miss Bradley and her brother. They sat on the wall and changed their footwear for ice skates with leather boots. Then they stepped onto the ice and skated; I had never seen anyone skating before, and this was really exciting! Anne and I watched for a few minutes and then became emboldened and made our way further out onto the ice ourselves, trying to imitate the skating movements of the Bradleys. We had to take care to remain on the ice at the lane end of the lake; it would probably not have been so safe at the other end by the rushes.

During the following week, people were talking about the frozen lake and the Bradleys skating on it. Several villagers spoke about the story of when the River Severn had frozen in Worcester, probably before the turn of the century, and people skated and walked over it on the ice. There was even a story about a horse and cart being driven over the ice and another about a burning brazier being taken onto it from which roasted chestnuts were sold. It never took long after events such as our frozen lake, for people to recall related stories from the past.

I understand that in 1820 the 14th of January was the coldest day of the year, when the temperature was recorded at −4°F. The River Thames in London froze in 1814 and crowds of people walked on the ice. "Opposite Queenhithe, where the mass appeared most solid, upwards of thirty booths were erected for the sale of liquors and viands, and for the playing of skittles. Musicians came, and people danced on the rough and slippery surface, (it is said that) . . . the scene was singularly cheerful and exciting."

(Quoted from "The English Year" by Roy Strong and Julia Trevelyan Oman).

After the war the young lady named Gwen Green who worked as an assistant at our shop, became engaged to Chuck Bull. When I was fourteen I joined the Old Time Dancing classes in the Memorial Hall and used to dance with Peter and Derek; we all enjoyed ourselves. Peter I remember as being shorter than his brothers, stocky with a slightly tubby figure, whereas Derek and Chuck had darker hair and were comparatively slim and certainly taller like their father. They were a nice well-mannered family who worked hard and were accepted by the villagers.

I have since been told that there was another, less romantic aspect of Turnmill; a group of young men used to arrange to meet there for *dogging* (watching the sexual activities of others). Village girls and their boyfriends walked down the lane and onto the tree-lined riverside meadows where they thought they had privacy for passionate interludes. No doubt the Yanks who came to the village were introduced to this beauty spot too.

There were plenty of opportunities for those voyeurs!

CHAPTER
TWENTY

Sodding Sid

Sid Robbins and his wife were family friends, who had a small farm near the village. I enjoyed calling there when I was in the van with Uncle John delivering groceries. Mrs. Robbins was quite a contrast to Sid, a quiet very well-spoken, respected lady. She had a kindly manner and smiling face and was a good customer at our shop. "Sodding Sid", as everyone knew him, had a broad country accent and a habit of peppering his conversation with the word "sodding". . ."Them sodding Gypos (gypsies) have been 'elping themselves from the store shed again!" Or "I've had a sodding fox at me chickens, I'll put some sodding lead into 'im, I'll get the b***** never you mind!" Sid had a great sense of humour and he loved a joke, he was also well liked and always had something to say to make people laugh.

I always enjoyed hearing Sid talk, and remember him touching his cap when he saw a magpie and saying "Good day Mr. Magpie", he believed this removed any risk of bad luck befalling him. Lots of people remembered, and passed on magpie superstition; in Devon they spit three times when they see the bird, to avoid bad luck. It is said that the magpie was not allowed into the Ark, but had to perch on the roof because of its incessant chattering. Shakespeare refers to the magpie . . .

> Augurs and understood relations have
> (By maggot pies, and choughs, and rooks) brought
>   forth
> The secret'st man of blood.
>
> *Macbeth III iv*

There are various regional versions of the "One for sorrow, two for joy, three for a girl and four for a boy" rhyme about the number of magpies seen in the course of a walk or journey. In the East the magpie is the Bird of Joy and good fortune, its chattering signifies good news and the arrival of guests. Much of the magpie superstition is thought to have stemmed from trench warfare in World War I. The magpie (Pica pica) is of the corvid family, who pick up bright objects and put them in their nests. When magpies and other corvids find dead or nearly dead animals or human bodies, they tend to go for the eyes first. To a soldier lying injured and helpless one magpie could be unlucky because it would have a clear field of attack, whereas two magpies would immediately begin to quarrel over the prey. In his book "Far from the Madding Crowd" (Ch.viii) Thomas Hardy wrote "What a night of horrors! I've seen a magpie all alone."

Sodding Sid had been trained as a baker and confectioner when he was young, and could make and ice the most wonderful cakes. He and his wife were often invited to our family parties, to which he usually brought a cake. His Christmas cakes were very good and decorated with hand-made marzipan fruits. He once made a lovely cake for Easter in the shape of a basket with open lid, the icing was made and coloured to look exactly like woven basket, and it was filled with hand-made edible spring flowers — he was an artist at his craft. He liked to join in when my aunt was playing the piano and we were all singing, he had quite a good voice and so did Mrs. Robbins.

CHAPTER
TWENTY-ONE

Mrs. Sanders and her Shop

Grandma often took me for a walk up the village to Mrs. Sanders's shop; it was a small shop with a small window, both were positively crammed with goods. Hers was a dolly-mixture of a shop, haberdashery, toys, clothing, household linens, greetings cards, wrapping paper, stationery items — all sorts of things were there.

When you opened the shop door a bell rang, and you stepped inside onto the wooden floor taking care not to tread on the stock. Piles of items had spilled over from the lower shelves, a colourful mixture of garments in all shapes and sizes hung from the ceiling. Mrs. Sanders, when not serving a customer, would emerge from her kitchen beyond the stock room at the rear of the shop. Smells of cooking and often clouds of steam wafted into the shop space. Mrs. Sanders and her husband lived above and at the rear of the narrow shop. Always clad in a floral cross-over apron (one of her best selling items) covering her clothes from shoulders to knees, she was a cheerful person, interested in her customers and usually ready to have a general chat. I was always fascinated at the higgledy-piggledy assortment of knitting wools, fabrics, patterns, cottons, embroidery silks and other things piled everywhere. Grandma bought wool for knitting socks from Mrs. Sanders.

Dolls in various sizes were on shelves at the back of the shop; some with hairless china heads and fabric stuffed bodies, golly-wogs, teddy bears, and a few other soft toys. Here too was a limited range of boxed games, tiddly-winks, snakes and ladders, draughts and jigsaws. Skipping ropes, rubber balls, marbles, kits for making model aeroplanes and tin clockwork toys. Another shelf displayed crayons and colouring books printed on cheap paper, and cheap story books. A better range of toys could be found in Worcester, but even so, the things children had then were very basic and unsophisticated.

Mrs. Sanders had a wonderful knack of changing the toy display in her window to comply with the seasons. As soon as the conker season was over she displayed things like marbles, yo-yos and rubber balls. That was followed by sparklers and fireworks for bonfire night. Children kept a close eye on that shop window and spent their little bits of saved earnings and pocket money there, often taking their new acquisitions to school to show to their friends — Mrs. Sanders always said "Show your friends and tell them you bought it from me."

The war years were a time for make-do-and-mend; mothers unpicked items of adult clothing to make clothes for themselves and the children. Old curtains, blankets and household linen were put to good use. They learned how to dye fabrics by boiling them with onion skins, coffee and beetroot or packets of powdered dye colours.

Some of the men put their hands to making wooden toys for birthday and Christmas presents for the children. Old toys such as dolls' prams, tricycles and bicycles were done up and passed from one owner to another.

When the fruit was ripe in summer time, Mrs. Sanders put up a table outside her shop, where she sold black and red currants, raspberries, strawberries, plums, damsons and apples. Sometimes her husband added salad vegetables to the display. A mother with a toddler in a pushchair was talking to someone outside Mrs. Sanders's shop one day, when the child took and ate a ripe plum from a box on the table, then just as it reached for another one, Mrs. Sanders appeared. She picked up the stone the child had thrown down and charged the mother a penny each for the two plums! The story was related in our shop, and they all said Mrs. S. was a mean old bat! She had several plum trees in her garden with lots of fruit on them and never missed an opportunity to make money.

CHAPTER
TWENTY-TWO

Mrs. Lee, Licensee of "The King's Arms"

The King's Arms public house was kept by a widow of ample proportions called Mrs. Lee. She came to the village from Birmingham after the death of her husband, with whom she ran a large public house in the suburbs between Longbridge and Five Ways. She brought her old mother to live with her and employed a man who lived in a cottage opposite the Crown & Sandys Hotel, who used to do all the cellar work and heavy jobs and ran the bar when needed. It was essential for her to have a man around, especially if there was trouble. When the gypsies were camped in the village, they came to the pub and sat outside at the back, but alcohol always made them quarrelsome, and sometimes the police were needed.

Mrs. Lee had a black spaniel dog called Lindy who I used to take for walks with our own spaniels. Her mother helped in the kitchen, especially when Mrs. Lee was preparing food for a special tea for the village cricket team. She also put on suppers for the bowling club gentlemen who played on the green at the back of the pub. My father used to play bowls there; it was a beautiful green with a wooden summerhouse at one end, and hazelnut trees frequented by squirrels when the nuts were ripe. There were also lilac trees around it and clusters of tall phlox flowers and Michaelmas-daisies.

Customers at the pub received a welcome from Mrs. Lee as she pulled pints of beer, served drinks and talked to everyone. In the warm weather her brightly printed cotton dresses had short sleeves, showing her big arms when she pulled the beer pumps.

Mrs. Lee sometimes wore a heavy silver charm bracelet. From almost every link hung large fascinating charms. She used to take it off for me when she was sitting outside having a rest, as she knew I loved looking at it and she could tell me a story about the charms and where they had come from. One of them was a Chinese pagoda with a jewel set in the top, given to her by a young man who was her sweetheart. Sadly he went away to fight in World War I and was killed. The castle charm was a gift from her husband when they were on their honeymoon at Great Yarmouth to remind her of the castle they built in the sand. He gave her another charm in the shape of a car he had owned in which they had lots of happy outings. She had others representing the zodiac signs for her own and the birthdays of relatives. All were beautifully made. I am sure the memories tied up with that piece of jewellery were more valuable to her than the bracelet. Mrs. Lee often leant out of her bedroom window talking to people walking by. She had a loud voice and laughed a lot, propping her large bust on the windowsill and holding conversations with people standing below.

It was said that when someone knocked on the front door early in the morning two heads would come out of the open window, Mrs. Lee and her cellar man!

"The King's Arms" was built in the 16th century and it is thought to contain evidence and relics of the time Charles II was fleeing from the Battle of Worcester, pausing there to rest and take sustenance before continuing his journey north.

CHAPTER
TWENTY-THREE

Charlie Morris

Next door to our shop was another shop owned by a family named Morris. They had a small tearoom and in the shop they sold paint, distemper, brushes, varnish, electrical plugs, light bulbs and an assortment of other items. They also had an ice cream freezer cabinet from which they sold ices. They kept a few flavours and scooped out the ice cream into cornets, always popular with the children when the weather was warm.

I particularly remember Charlie Morris, the unmarried son of the family, who lived there and served in the shop. Charlie had a very exuberant personality. He was a tall slim man with thick wavy brown hair and a moustache, who always seemed to be full of fun, laughed a lot and had twinkling eyes.

"What ho, young Rosie!" He would say as I entered the shop. He used words and phrases such as "spiffing", "whacko" "jolly good show" and "absolutely top hole don't you know!"

Charlie was always laughing and cracking jokes. He had joined the Home Guard and must have been a great chap to be with, always creating plenty of laughs.

He also took part in the village concert party, where he was a great asset to the show; a natural on stage.

Charlie wore tweeds, bright coloured ties and Fair Isle patterned pullovers. He looked very smart in his brown tweed plus-fours when going off to play golf at Droitwich. He drove a car, always kept clean and shining, and would call and wave to people as he drove by, sometimes throwing out his right arm to wave and call out "Wotcha!" or "Steady past yer Grannies!" and other cheery greetings.

CHAPTER
TWENTY-FOUR

Frank and Jinny Perkins

I knew them as Mr. and Mrs. Perkins, who had a small sweet shop and barber's shop close to the weigh-bridge by the main road island. Their premises was known as "The Old Post Office". Mrs. Perkins kept the sweet shop where large jars of boiled sweets stood along the counter and boxes of chocolate bars, liquorice sticks and sherbet bags stood on the shelves at the back. The little shop had a very small window and was dimly lit, the wooden floor was dark and the ceiling low. Mrs. Perkins was kind, smiling and always ready to help anyone with a problem.

Mr. Perkins had many skills — he was the village barber who cut my father's hair, a thatcher and a hedger and ditcher.

Thatcher.

Bespoke for weeks, he turned up some morning
Unexpectedly, his bicycle slung
With a light ladder and a bag of knives.
He eyed the old rigging, poked at the eaves,

Opened and handled sheaves of lashed wheat-
    straw,
Next, the bundled rods: hazel and willow
Were flicked for weight, twisted in case they'd
    snap.
It seemed he spent the morning warming up:

Then fixed the ladder, laid out well-honed blades
And snipped at straw and sharpened ends of rods
That, bent in two, made a white pronged staple
For pinning down his world, handful by handful.

Couchant for days on sods above the rafters
He shaved and flushed the butts, stitched all
    together
Into a sloped honeycomb, a stubble patch,
And left them gaping at his Midas touch.
              Seamus Heaney 1939 —

One day when the leaves had fallen from the trees, I was walking along Sinton Lane with my friend Janet. We were going for a walk in "The Big Wood", one of our favourite places. It is a very old oak woodland more correctly known as "Knight's Grove", belonging to the Sandys Estate, dating back to very early times when the country was mainly covered by forest.

There, on the side of the lane we met Mr. Perkins, who had cleaned out the ditch running by the lane and was laying the hedge. He was sitting on the bank by the hedge eating his bread and cheese; slicing off pieces of cheese with his penknife and tearing chunks of bread

177

from the end of a loaf wrapped in a cloth. He greeted us both by name, smiling, and saying "Hello Rosie and Janet, where are you girls going?" "We want to see if there are any acorns left in the Big Wood" we replied. "You sit here by me and I'll tell you something about that wood and this part of the Estate." He patted the smooth bank at his side as he spoke. We sat beside him, always ready to hear him talk, as he told us interesting things, and made us laugh. When he had taken a drink from the bottle of cold tea at his side, he said, "I know you girls like the wood, it's a real old wood to be sure."

We heard gun-shots, and Mr. Perkins said, "That'll be them silly buggers I saw last week, they're pigeon shooting. Last Saturday I was down at 'Hadley Bowling Green' (a public house a short distance away). I was there to see about a job. Them chaps had been there until the Landlord closed at two o'clock, they came out shouting, laughing, throwing their hats into the air and firing shots at 'em. One chap fell over, they pulled him up but he'd had one over the eight of the ale or cider — silly buggers!"

We enjoyed talking to Mr. Perkins, who told us about the old hedge he way laying, which had hawthorn, hazel, elm and elderberry in it. He was cleaning off a pile of young sticks and laying them on a piece of sacking in a neat bundle. He told us they would be useful for thatching, and he had just had an order for a new thatch. He had put some old birds' nests taken from that stretch of hedge on one side, and said birds like to be near to cornfields, adding that the pond, in one corner of the field behind the hedge, was a source of water for them too. We examined the nests, and he told us what type of birds had built them; some of them had a smooth mud lining, others had soft hair, sheep wool and feather linings. The newly laid stretch of hedge looked so good, all neatly entwined with new stakes at intervals, all the briars and climbing weeds removed. He told us that the new stakes very often took root and became a growing part of the hedge. Two old stakes had become blackthorn trees in the hedge, which had been cut into shape and left to grow; Mr. Perkins told us that he knew people who liked to pick the sloes for making sloe gin, saying we may get to taste some when we were older.

When he stood up Mr. Perkins stretched and yawned, then he invited us to follow him to the pond. He was complaining about having to clean it out, but when we got nearer we could see how overgrown it had become. He was not looking forward to that job, but the farmer wanted it cleared out and had offered him good money for the whole job. Mr. Perkins told us that when he had finished cutting back the undergrowth around the pond and had cleared the banks and pulled out lots of the weed, we would be able to see the clear water from the spring below. He said that we would see wagtails, even kingfishers by the old pond and there would be more newts and sticklebacks there too.

Frank Perkins was a man who really enjoyed his work and loved working on his own in the countryside which he knew so well.

CHAPTER
TWENTY-FIVE

Dorothy and her Jackdaw

My friend Dorothy, four years my senior, lived mostly with her grandparents Mr. and Mrs. Perkins and was almost like an older sister to me. Dorothy was always very good with horses and had a way with most animals and wild creatures. One year she found a young jackdaw with a broken leg. It was a fledgling in a sorry state, and its plumage was brownish at this stage. Dorothy took it home and with her grandfather's help she fixed a splint to the broken leg. They called him "Jack" and made him a rough wooden cage placed by the kitchen door; the cage, with a wire netting door at the front and straw on the bottom suited him well. They quickly found they could leave the front of the cage open in the daytime, and he would flutter down and get himself around, often being shooed out of the house by Granny Perkins. Jack soon began to explore beyond their small garden. Soon, as he grew into an adult bird, his feathers became mainly black with grey patches on the cheeks and nape of the neck; the black feathers on his crown, wings and tail glossed with light-catching blues and greens. Jack's leg grew stronger and he developed quite a personality. He learned to say

"Hello Jack" and understood Dorothy when she said "Scratch yer nobby Jack" — he would lower his head and enjoy the attention. At dusk he would always get back into his cage and they fastened the door to keep him safe during the night.

One Sunday we were all in the church for the Harvest Thanksgiving service; the church was beautifully decorated with sheaves of corn, flowers, vegetables and fruit. The organ was playing, the choir and congregation had just finished one of the hymns and when everyone was seated the vicar was climbing up into the pulpit to deliver his sermon. Before he reached the top step, Jack entered the church and came hopping up the aisle calling his name loudly. Everyone laughed, and undaunted Jack reached the lectern, hopping and fluttering up via the corn sheaf and vegetables placed around it. Standing there looking down at the congregation he fluttered his wings and opened his beak to repeat another loud "Jack". At this point the verger, Wilf Dyson, came after him, but Jack thought it was all a good game, and flew down onto the pews making his way around the church, calling his name with glee and getting Wilf very hot under the collar! Dorothy left her seat and went to the church door and was there to receive him as he was driven out. If Wilf had asked her sooner, they would have had much less "entertainment" as he always came when Dorothy called him to sit on her arm.

The winter came, and Jack was excited by the snow; I had made a snowman on our lawn, and Jack sat on top of it and flapped his wings, making loud calls. He

181

was funny on the ice, he skidded and flapped around making us children laugh.

Jack became well known in the village — he would poke his cheeky head around any door. One day he returned home in a dreadful state; he had been in the Police Sergeant's chicken run where two young cockerels set about him. Poor Jack, he was making an awful noise and was covered in mud and unable to fly up to his cage.

Dorothy and her grandparents attended to him, saying that they doubted whether he would last the night. Next day, he was there resting on his straw and opened a bright eye when Dorothy came to see him. He got to his feet, had a good shake and was ready for some food. He had such spirit, it would take more than a couple of cockerels to get the better of him!

Jack often picked up bright objects he found lying around and placed them in his cage, like magpies do, taking their finds to the nest. His territory widened and soon he was going to the village school, where in summer time he found classroom doors open. He delighted the children by strolling in, calling his name and hopping up onto the desks. The teachers and headmaster were not amused by his disruptive influence on their classes!

Unfortunately for the gregarious Jack, his school visits brought about his end. One day he returned home looking and sounding very unwell, making the most alarming noise, and flopped down. There was nothing they could do to save him, he was dead. Dorothy and her grandparents were sure that he had been given some poison up at the school. Dorothy was broken hearted and everyone was sad when they heard of his untimely demise; he had won friends wherever he went and was sadly missed — he certainly earned his place in communal memory.

CHAPTER
TWENTY-SIX

Molly Butler

Molly lived with her mother in a 16th century thatched cottage in the centre of the village. Granny Butler kept a small tea-room and offered bed and breakfast to visitors. The cottage had plenty of ground around it. Molly was a hard-working, strong woman, out in all weathers tending her animals. She dressed accordingly; I can see her now striding along in her heavy shoes or boots with an old felt hat pulled well down on her head. She usually wore a brown overall covering her body to just above the knees. She often wore trousers, but sometimes the hem of a skirt could be seen below her overall; in wet weather she donned a greasy old waterproof coat which just covered the tops of her black Wellington boots.

If I went up to the hedge at the back of our School Bank garden, I could look through and see Molly at work mucking out or feeding her pigs. There was always a lot of noise from them at feeding time, as they enjoyed the vegetable waste and windfall fruit as well as the cereal mash she mixed up for them. Molly also kept chickens, and sometimes she had a lamb or two to fatten up, which would be moved around to keep the grass down and were no doubt sold to a butcher for slaughter when fully grown. She worked on their sizeable vegetable patch, growing legumes, brassicas and root vegetables, for their own use and to sell. She dug and weeded the ground and did all the work necessary to produce and harvest her vegetables. The orchard contained a mixture of fruit trees, which she tended and harvested single-handed.

I remember hearing about one hot summer day when the plums were ripe, Molly was up a ladder picking them, she felt thirsty and took a bite into a juicy plum. Unfortunately there was a wasp in it and it stung her inside her throat, which was alarming and painful for her, and she was rushed to hospital. News of her sudden misadventure spread around the village. She recovered from that experience very quickly and was soon back again working away as usual.

Water for the home, garden and animals had to be drawn from a well via a hand pump near to the cottage. Molly carried it in large buckets, and people passing by the cottage would frequently see Molly with a bucket in each hand carting water from the pump.

Molly enjoyed her cigarettes, and she liked to have a bet on the horses. She made regular visits to the village telephone box to lay on her bets with a bookmaker. She didn't have much of a social life, perhaps she enjoyed a drink of beer or cider at the pub, I don't know; to me it seemed she didn't have time for anything except work. Hers was a productive way of life, she certainly did her bit for the war effort.

CHAPTER
TWENTY-SEVEN

Arnold Reynolds

Picture a tall, thin, round-shouldered man who walked with long strides, often wearing a long, dark overcoat or a long beige raincoat flapping around his legs. He walked about two and a half miles from his home to our shop, and on arriving he always removed his hat. He greeted whoever stood behind the counter in his quiet way, enquiring about ourselves. Usually he was glad to sit down and, once settled on a chair, he ran his hands through his thick, greying, brown curly hair and entered into conversation about the latest news, the war, the weather and what he had been doing since he last visited the shop. He always had a list of his requirements ready and we all liked to listen to him talk. We called him "Mr. Arnold" and he sometimes told us about his latest trip to London; he used to live and work there before he retired. He was an artist, and spent most of his time drawing and painting. He sometimes took his work to a private gallery in London where it was sold.

My friend Anne and I sometimes walked to his home, and once when he was unwell in the school holidays he telephoned the shop to ask for some things.

As it was not a big order and we were there playing in the garden, we were asked to take it to him. This we gladly did, and when we arrived he let us in and explained that he was suffering from his "old trouble" which would pass now he had the medicine sent to him via the District Nurse. Mother said he had spent many years in the tropics and continued to have bouts of a complaint contracted there. His home was located between the village and the River Severn; the living room was quite large and had a lovely big window opening out onto a wooden balcony; from there he could see across the river to rolling fields, copses and large trees.

Although the day was warm and we were in our cotton dresses, he was wrapped in his long thick dressing gown over his shirt and trousers. He invited us to sit down and brought us drinks of squash and a little plate of biscuits. We were so interested in all the strange and exotic things hanging on the walls, and he enjoyed showing them to us and telling us where he had been when he acquired them. He had a gramophone with a wide-rimmed brass sound trumpet on the top, and a violin.

We were invited to return on another day, as he said he liked talking to us. He showed us his camera and photographs he had taken and used to compose his drawings and paintings. He did some drawings with pens and ink, then he delicately enhanced them using touches of delicate water-colour paint. His big folio of paintings and drawings of his times in far-off lands was our favourite, because he told us all kinds of things about his experiences.

Mr. Arnold showed us how he made his own paints by crushing lumps of various minerals using a muller to make powders of different colours which he then mixed with oil. One day he took us to a small wooded area at the end of his garden, and told us to search around to find some thing we could draw. I found a big snail and Anne found a piece of wood with fungus growing from it. Back on his veranda he provided us with paper and small drawing boards and left us to it for a while. He came back with a dead crow and told us about them and their habits. He loved teaching us things about the wildlife around us. He placed the dead bird on the table and stretched out a wing into a fully spread position, tying it with string, showing us the bone structure and arrangement of large primary feathers and talking about bird flight; his drawing of the wing was *wonderful*. He told us to begin with the basic shape of the object then to pinpoint the position of the main features before concentrating on finer detail and above all to keep looking and drawing; he assured us that the more we practiced the better we would get — he was a good teacher. We always went home with things to show and plenty to talk about after we had spent some time with Mr. Arnold.

CHAPTER
TWENTY-EIGHT

Mrs. Joan and Mr. Edgar

A retired couple who were customers at our shop were known to us as Mrs. Joan and Mr. Edgar; theirs was a very nice house set in lovely gardens with an orchard not far from the centre of the village. They loved their garden, and certainly spent a lot of time working outside. It was their paradise. They grew soft fruits, and sold them along with fruit from the trees in their orchard. Mrs. Joan made jams, jellies and preserves; they were always busy. One of their greatest interests was bee keeping, and I remember taking an errand to them, when they were by the beehives, both wearing their apiarists' hats and veils.

They had a number of hives in their orchard, which were the multiple storey box hives, designed by an American named Moses Quinby, who also invented the smoker used to pacify the bees. They always invited me into their kitchen and gave me a drink and a biscuit. They talked to me about their bees, telling me that a beehive is like a living body with all organs working to sustain it. The bees transmit information to each other about food sources by a "dance"; each movement gives out sound impulses which are picked up by tiny hairs on the back of the bee's head. The bees know how to orientate this "dance" and use the sun to find their way around.

Mrs. Joan and Mr. Edgar told me that bees know when anything is wrong or threatening around, and let their keepers know because they become disturbed. Bees are normally calm, and if a bee flies around a human, it is not intending to sting the person, unless it senses a threat of some kind. (Melitin, an extract of honeybee poison, has been developed as a vaccine treatment and is now used as a powerful antibiotic). Mrs. Joan and Mr. Edgar made lovely honey and brought jars of it each year for us to sell in the shop. I was fascinated to see how they emptied the honeycombs and filtered the honey to clear it of impurities; in those days it was a laborious process, but they enjoyed collecting and bottling up their honey harvest.

Then we heard the surprising news that Mr. Edgar had been found dead in the orchard. We were shocked at hearing he had committed suicide, and that Mrs. Joan found him. He had taken his loaded gun, put the end of the barrel into his mouth and pulled the trigger. I was so sorry that Mrs. Joan found him like that; their bees must have been very upset, even swarming because it occurred so close to their hives. We later heard that he had lost a lot of money speculating with stocks and shares. The house was sold and Mrs. Joan moved away.

POSTSCRIPT

That is how I heard the news of Mr. Edgar's death as a child, no doubt the family knew more. I discovered many years later that he was in fact an accountant who looked after people's finances and investments. He had embezzled a large sum of money from a local farmer, who went to his bank one day and discovered money had been taken from his account. He took immediate legal action No doubt Mr. Edgar heard about this very quickly, and for him it was the tip of the iceberg. He knew what was coming, his life was in ruins; prosecution and prison loomed large, so he reached for his gun.

CHAPTER
TWENTY-NINE

Captain "Dick" Warren

Captain Warren came to live in Ombersley in the year the war ended. He had been Captain of luxury passenger liners before the war began. He took passengers on cruises to the Far East and beyond, his charming wife Gwen travelled with him and they enjoyed that privileged style of life for many years. Gwen had relatives living in our village, and we occasionally saw them when they came for brief visits before the war.

Soon after the war began some cruise liners were commandeered for war service, and Captain Dick was given the job of running one which had been adapted to transport armaments. Mrs. Gwen came to the village often to stay with her family, and was also doing a job somewhere in the Home Counties to help with the war effort. "Uncle Dick" as I knew him, continually ran his ship, travelling across oceans with cargoes of weapons, explosives and military equipment. His ship was a target for enemy attack by submarines, other vessels and aircraft fire. The strain of being in this very risky situation for several years must have been considerable for him and his crew.

When the war ended he and his wife found a house to rent in the middle of the village and they came to live quietly and enjoy the peace and quiet of rural England.

All was not well however Uncle Dick was going through a bad phase, probably a nervous breakdown; he was drinking heavily. I used to call in to see him sometimes, and was intrigued by the smell of the spicy curries he made for himself. Villagers who caught a whiff of his cooking were heard to make scathing comments about it — oriental cuisine was eschewed by them, even though most people had not tasted anything but traditional English cooking. I used to run errands for him and I remember him telling me to pick fruit from his garden if my family could use any of it. He took no interest in the large walled garden at the rear of their home. I became quite fond of him, as he was always kind to me, and I found his descriptions of places and people he remembered from his Eothen (Eastern) travels and experiences at sea before the war fascinating. I think he enjoyed responding to my childish questions about the exotic places he had known. He showed me photographs from a beautiful carved wooden camphor chest in which he kept some of his treasures. He had a wonderful intricately carved ivory chess set, which I used to love to handle and examine the chessmen.

His wife finally left him, he was hitting the bottle heavily and becoming increasingly depressed. Sadly he took his own life, a tragic end for a courageous officer and gentleman.

CHAPTER
THIRTY

Mrs. Davis

Mrs. Davis was an old widow lady who I met but never really knew. She used to come into our shop in the cold weather and was glad to sit down, get her breath back and warm up by the paraffin heater. She seemed to have plenty to moan about and rarely smiled. I remember a day when she was there moaning about her roof leaking and being unable to carry a bucket of water to her cottage from her pump. The hand pump for Mrs. Davis's cottage was at the end of Hilltop Lane near to the garages Uncle John used for his car and van. She had to walk down a narrow dirt pathway from her cottage (roughly 30–40 yards) to get her buckets of water.

I used to pass by her cottage often when I went up the lane and across a field to get to School Bank, an alternative route I enjoyed, especially if I had been playing with my friend Janet Wood who lived in Hilltop House. The narrow pathway ran close to the back wall of Mrs. Davis's cottage, where there was not a door or window in the wall. On one summer's day I had to take something up to Mrs. Davis from the shop, so I went through the little gate at the far side of her cottage and round to her front door. The garden was overgrown and neglected. I noticed that the cottage had two small windows at each side of the door on the ground floor, and three windows upstairs. She probably had two bedrooms and a small landing area. Mrs. Davis came to the door when I knocked, and asked me in. I found myself in a room which was both living room and kitchen; a staircase at the back led to the bedrooms.

That old cottage was built to a very simple design. Mrs. Davis had a small cast iron coal and wood burning range for cooking and heating the room. She had no electricity, her only source of light was by paraffin lamps and candles; she probably had paraffin stoves for additional heat. She had no bathroom and her lavatory was outside not far from the single doorway into the only ground floor room. On that day the blossom from the flowering currant bush by her lavatory was pretty but always gave off a strong smell of cats' pee.

In her room there were bunches of dried herbs hanging from a beam in the ceiling, and a large table in the centre half covered with a chenille cloth. A brass-based oil lamp stood in the middle of the table, and the mantelpiece over the black range had a tasselled fringe around it with colourful china ornaments standing at each end and a clock in the middle. Basic wooden chairs stood by the table and an old armchair by the fire with hand-crocheted rug over it.

The red brick floor had a threadbare square of carpet covering the centre of the room and by the fire there was an old, handmade rag rug. The room was very dark even on a sunny day but I did notice other things, one or two pictures on the wall, a little bookcase with books and boxes on it, framed photographs and a large old family Bible were placed on a chest of drawers under window. She didn't have much to say to me, I think she was feeling poorly.

Later that year, Mrs. Davis became housebound and neighbours, who lived in the separate front section of Hilltop House, fetched her oil and firewood and carried her water. Then came the sad day when my mother and I walked down past her cottage and found all her furniture, goods and chattels piled up at the top of the lane by the pump. Mother said old Mrs. Davis must be dead. The small open-topped boxes of clothing, shoes, linen, bits of china, and utensils, a couple of framed pictures, saucepans and enamel bowls, were stacked under the table. I spotted her framed photographs and family Bible. That pathetic pile of worldly possessions gave such a clear picture of that poor woman. Mrs. Davis had lived a very simple life without any of the paraphernalia needed even then to create a feeling of domestic comfort enjoyed by most. Her life must have been very lonely after the death of her husband.

We went to her funeral. I can't remember how old Mrs. Davis was, but I do remember standing outside the church afterwards, listening to Mother's conversations with people who had known her. One man said how well the Davises used to keep their garden, — Mr. Davis was known as a good gardener. Someone else talked about Mrs. Davis's preserves — her jams, jellies and pickles were sought-after at the annual fête.

We learned that Mrs. Davis was also remembered for her knowledge of wild plants and that she could make up herbal medicines. Village folk sometimes visited her, because her remedies for common complaints were known to be efficacious. No doubt the stale overdried bunches of herbs which hung from her living room ceiling had remained there as a reminder of her more active life.

So ended the life of a humble woman who had known only a simple way of country life. Going to church was probably the highlight of her week, especially after the death of her husband. There were many such people then, who had nothing, whose expectations didn't go beyond a roof over their heads, a bed to sleep on, table and chairs and a seat by the fire. They were largely self-sufficient with the produce of their gardens and the countryside around them. It was not unusual to meet old people who had never travelled to the nearest big town. When they visited friends or received visitors, they would sit around telling old stories passed on through their families. Family bibles were treasured possessions because they contained dates of births, marriages and deaths, some documents of land and property, portrait drawings, and even early photographs of the family. Other mementoes such as hand-embroidered specimen pieces made by young girls for special occasions, invitation cards, birthday and valentine cards were also saved in these great books.

197

Epilogue

My story of that seemingly transient period cannot be completed without unfolding a less than happy sequence of events for me and my family. In 1949 I was twelve years old and left the village school, transferring to a school in Worcester. I travelled to school by bus each day with many of my village friends. My father had not been well and at long last the doctor sent him to the Worcester hospital for some X-rays and examination. He was told he had a tumour and would be admitted for immediate surgery. I remember vividly visiting him after his operation and standing by my mother at the end of the ward with the ward sister telling us that Daddy's operation had revealed that the cancerous growth was so widespread that surgery was impossible. The surgeon had merely stitched up the incision and they intended to send him home as soon as possible; he was not expected to live more than three months. The long surgical incision down his abdomen would not heal; he was kept in hospital for longer than expected. Then he was sent home, and the village doctor and village nurse began calling. At first he was eager to get up and about, he thought he had been through a successful operation and was on the road to recovery. I returned from school one day and found him turning over a patch of the garden with a fork. I hurried into the house and went to my room to cry.

That burst of "normality" was short lived, as Daddy soon became weak and bedridden. The doctor did what he could using barbiturate pain killers, and the district nurse called regularly to care for him. He lived for six months after being admitted to the hospital. I spent quite a lot of time with Grandma and lived at the shop; Grandma was always pleased to have me there and it was certainly good that my little bedroom was always there for me. Mother was constantly involved with nursing my father and felt that it was better for me to be away from the constant reminder of his painful demise.

I was invited to tea with Anne Sapsford and her family on Sundays, and I visited other friends in the village after school, on Saturdays and during holidays. Christmas was a sad time. On Christmas morning I went to School Bank to take my mother her present and to see Daddy. I asked if I should take him some of the "Churchmans" cigarettes which he always smoked, but was told not to do so, so I bought him boiled sweets. He was unable to join in any Christmas spirit, and I couldn't show him gifts I had received, as his pain was severe, especially when the effects of his medication wore off. His last days were filled with cries of pain, delirious ramblings and finally a period of coma induced by doses of barbiturates until his death. I was not allowed to attend his funeral; Mother had arranged for him to be cremated in Cheltenham and attended his funeral alone in the spring of 1950.

Mother then had to do something to increase her income, she couldn't afford to keep me, pay the rent and overheads with only her small wage from the shop. So she took in a lodger, a young lady teacher who had recently been appointed at the village school. She was a pleasant person and was engaged to marry a blind man to whom she wrote letters in braille. After a time she left to move nearer to her fiancé and we had another young unmarried lady teacher named Evelyn as our lodger.

I left school and attended the Technical Collage for a year to take a Secretarial course, then I worked as a shorthand typist in Worcester. Grandma was no longer able to do all the cooking at the shop, and was eager to move away. She and my mother talked it over and decided to buy a large Victorian house in Worcester, we left the village in 1954. Our lady teacher lodger came with us, I continued to do office work and Mother looked after Gran and took two gentlemen lodgers as well, to make ends meet. One lodger named George brought a television set with him and we had it in the sitting room, which I enjoyed. We never owned a TV ourselves; Aunty Win and Uncle John had one at the shop, I remember seeing the 1953 Coronation on it. The six bedroomed semi-detached house had a good sized bathroom and a separate toilet upstairs, and another flush toilet on the ground floor. I liked living there.

Grandma died in 1955, aged 82, and the family turned up for the funeral. My mother's brother Gilbert and sister Gladys and their spouses came as well as Aunty Win and Uncle John. There were a lot of questions being asked about where Mother got the money from to buy the house, and how much money had Gran left, and who was going to have pieces of her furniture which she brought with her. Mother tried to keep me out of all that. It seemed very unpleasant, and they had never told me much about family affairs — "children should be seen and not heard" was their approach.

The house we were living in was sold, the remnants of our furniture put in store, and Mother bought a two up and two down country cottage, with no plumbing. Aunty Win and Uncle John decided to buy a house in Worcester, and they took on a couple to live and run the shop. Uncle John drove to Ombersley every day to work at the shop. I was aware that Aunty Win was feeling unsettled; Mother and I stayed with them in Worcester while Mother was waiting to take over the cottage. I came home from the office one day and found Aunty unconscious on their bed after taking an overdose of tablets. I pulled her up on the bed and tried to revive her, but could do nothing. I rushed downstairs, picked up the telephone and was trying to get through to their doctor, when Uncle John came home, rushed upstairs to look at her, and took over. That was a big shock for me, but Aunty Win recovered from that suicide attempt and we moved into the tiny country cottage.

That was when I had to give up my job and find another one in the nearest town, Kidderminster. I travelled to work every day by bus, and disliked the job in the office of a very bad tempered solicitor. The village we had moved to hadn't any amenities to speak of, and there was very little for young people to do in their spare time. The novelty of drawing water from the shared well by bucket and handle soon wore off, the lack of plumbing was sadly missed by me, and I certainly didn't like having to take a bath on the kitchen floor with water heated in the electric boiler. The cottage was situated close to a hill and the mist and damp seemed to descend around me on winter mornings as I stood at the roadside waiting for the eight o'clock bus. I caught heavy coughs and colds and often felt really poorly. Mother listened to me coughing all night, but never suggested sending for a doctor.

During the three years when Mother and I lived at that cottage, I was told that Aunty Win's depression had increased, and she went to stay with her sister Gladys in Birmingham. Aunty Glad and Uncle Den were sympathetic and wanted to do all they could for her. One day while she was there Aunty Glad suggested going into the city for shopping and lunch. Aunty Win said she didn't feel like going out, so she was left alone in the large house in Oxford Road, Moseley. When Aunty Glad returned she found her lying on the bathroom floor having swallowed a quantity of poisonous lavatory cleaning fluid. She did all she could to get her unconscious sister to swallow some black coffee, but that was almost impossible. She sent for an ambulance, but Aunty Win couldn't be saved and died in hospital. Some fifteen years later I was told that her suicide was the only way she could end the pain of a broken heart caused by Uncle John's affair with another woman in Ombersley. My mother attended her funeral at Ombersley church.

After that sad event, Mother sold the cottage and we moved back to Worcester in 1958. Mother bought a small terraced house in Barbourne, we were very comfortable there, with a nice bathroom, a ground floor toilet, and a warm kitchen with a solid fuel boiler heating the water. I lost no time finding a secretarial job, and found a new friend next door; her name was Jill, she and her husband were living with her parents and she was expecting a baby. Then Jill's brother Bill came home from serving with the RAF in Singapore, we were introduced, fell in love and married in 1960. We have two children, now independent adults, one granddaughter, and continue to enjoy our lives together.

Five Minutes Love

Carol Hathorne

Carol Hathorne's nostalgic look at growing up in the West Midlands in the 1950s

I lay for a long time, listening to the sounds of the house gradually changing around me — the closing of doors and the switching off of lights. Warmth and security washed over me.

The first part, *Slurry and Strawberries*, tells of life on Tipton's Lost City Estate. The early and junior school years of a working class upbringing depict the warmth of family life set against a backdrop of social deprivation.

Bread Pudding Days moves the story on to senior school, travelling to Wednesbury, broadening horizons, new friends and old truths. *A Woodbine on the Wall* covers the rite of passage era in which a young woman and a writer emerges.

ISBN 978-0-7531-9474-4 (hb)
ISBN 978-0-7531-9475-1 (pb)

Little Apples Will Grow Again

Fred Brown

Even in the snow and ice of winter, when snowballs flew, and cold and busy gloved and ungloved hands patted snowmen into shape, the parents and grandparents would gather, shiver and talk about the weather.

Fred Brown recounts his own boisterous childhood, and the earlier life of his parents, Syd and Mary. They met whilst both in service and, despite struggling with Syd's depression, raised a large family.

With five brothers and a younger sister, Fred's early years were full of noise and mischief. Whilst fraught with terror for the adults, the war provided numerous distractions for the boys, from air raids to collecting shrapnel. This, along with joining one of the gangs that roamed the surrounding streets, meant that the children were always occupied.

ISBN 978-0-7531-9462-1 (hb)
ISBN 978-0-7531-9463-8 (pb)

Bockety

Desmond Ellis

The only people who aren't bockety are the ones who don't worry about anything. And the only people who don't worry about anything are simple-minded, and you can't get more bockety than that, can you?

Born in 1944, Desmond Ellis grew up on the banks of the Grand Canal in Dublin. This slightly awkward first-born child romps through his childhood like a bockety bicycle that won't quite go where it is steered. His playground is the Grand Canal, where he goes crashing through the reeds with fishing nets. At home he washes off the inevitable grime in a tin tub by the fire, and the toilet is a draughty shed in the yard.

Bockety is a tale of a time of few cars and many bicycles. Gratification was to be had in Cleeve's toffe and gobstoppers. And then there was the terrible confusion of girls . . .

ISBN 978-0-7531-9424-9 (hb)
ISBN 978-0-7531-9425-6 (pb)

Huddersfield at War

Hazel Wheeler

Many neighbours arranged to dash into each other's shelters on alternate alerts. It gave them a bit more chance to gossip.

Hazel Wheeler looks at life in Huddersfield during the Second World War. From rationing and the extra work that this involved for her shopkeeper father, to the working lives of men and women, this is an absorbing look at how the people of Huddersfield coped with the war. With a real sense of a community banding together, Hazel collects wartime stories of playing games while waiting for the all clear, of knitting for the troops and of the joy of VE day.

ISBN 978-0-7531-9416-4 (hb)
ISBN 978-0-7531-9417-1 (pb)

Northern Roots

Rod Broome

Much amusement was caused throughout the family when I went to Nurse Ellis's house to order a baby for Mum and Dad.

Rod Broome traces his northern roots in this charming memoir. Born in Lancashire in 1937, Rod was the treasured only child in a close extended family. He was to remain the centre of attention until his sister Maureen was born seven years later. His childhood was one of playing draughts with his grandad, keeping hens with his father and playing games in the street with his friends.

He talks about his family, his growing interest in nature and photography and his time at grammar school. After leaving school, Rod did his national service in the army, before training to be a teacher.

ISBN 978-0-7531-9398-3 (hb)
ISBN 978-0-7531-9399-0 (pb)

ISIS publish a wide range of books in large print, from fiction to biography. Any suggestions for books you would like to see in large print or audio are always welcome. Please send to the Editorial Department at:

ISIS Publishing Limited
7 Centremead
Osney Mead
Oxford OX2 0ES

A full list of titles is available free of charge from:

Ulverscroft Large Print Books Limited

(UK)
The Green
Bradgate Road, Anstey
Leicester LE7 7FU
Tel: (0116) 236 4325

(Australia)
P.O. Box 314
St Leonards
NSW 1590
Tel: (02) 9436 2622

(USA)
P.O. Box 1230
West Seneca
N.Y. 14224-1230
Tel: (716) 674 4270

(Canada)
P.O. Box 80038
Burlington
Ontario L7L 6B1
Tel: (905) 637 8734

(New Zealand)
P.O. Box 456
Feilding
Tel: (06) 323 6828

Details of **ISIS** complete and unabridged audio books are also available from these offices. Alternatively, contact your local library for details of their collection of **ISIS** large print and unabridged audio books.